Kent State Murder Day
May 4, 1970

Richard Del Connor

Shaolin Communications

Richard Del Connor

Kent State Murder Day

Richard Del Connor

Also by Richard Del Connor

4 Decades of Love
4 Noble Truths Explained by Buddha Z
5 Souls of God — Everyone is One of Five
7 Days in NoHo
12 Laws of Life — To Achieve Your Full Capability
Act Zen to Be Zen
Autumn Flavours - First of Four Seasons
Bat Cave Gold Mine
Buddha Kung Fu Student Manual
Connor Black Hole Bubble Theory
Coyote in a Graveyard
Coyote in a Graveyard NoHo — Homeless Shelter Evolution of a Shaolin Monk
Fistula of Fury
History of Zen from A to Z
Human Values for Success in Family and Business
Kent State Murder Day
Kung Fu Cowboy 1976
Kung Fu Cowboy: Zombie Killer
Love, Always & Forever!
Masonic Kung Fu
Philosopher Poet in a Field of Dreams
The Potatoe Valentine & Other Love Poems
Rainbow in the Shade
Season of Fours
Secret Gospel of Jamez
Shaolin Kung Fu Initiate
Shaolin Kung Fu Beginner
Sid's Place
Spring Fevers
Summer Forevers
Supersoul 13
Tai Chi Beginner Class Reading Manual (2008)
Tai Chi Intermediate
Tao of Taoism
Times Interview of Richard Del Connor
Utah Phase 1
Zen Spirit Book

Richard Del Connor

Kent State Murder Day
May 4, 1970
by Richard Del Connor, "The Hippy Coyote"

Published by *Shaolin Communications*

publisher@shaolinCOMMUNICATIONS.com (The Publisher)

© Copyright 2019 *shaolinMUSIC.com* All rights reserved. ASCAP

This book, or parts of this book, may not be reproduced in any form without written permission from the publisher. All lyrics included within this book are licensed and used by permission of Shaolin Music and Shaolin Records. For permission to use, publish, or license any of the songs, poems, photography, graphics or sentences of this book, contact The Publisher.

Edited and typeset by Richard Del Connor.
Photography, artworks and graphics by The Hippy Coyote.
Cover art: Richard Del Connor, The Hippy Coyote
Additional photos by permission of Kent State University Archive.-

All songs and lyrics in this book were written and composed by Richard Del Connor and copyrighted, published or released in various formats under pseudonyms: The Coyote, or The Hippy Coyote.

All songs in this book are copyright managed and owned by Shaolin Music. Shaolin Music is owned by Richard Del Connor and founded in 1984 along with Shaolin Records, the independent record label company of Richard. Shaolin Music is an ASCAP music publisher.

Lyrics and poems are used and printed with permission of Shaolin Music. *www.ShaolinMusic.com*

Author: Richard Del Connor
Musician artist name: 1984 to 2006 = The Coyote;
                2007 to 2014 = The Hippy Coyote
Chinese name: Zhen, Shen-Lang = Shen-Lang Zhen, "Buddha Zhen"
English translation of Chinese name: Spirit Wolf of Truth

Richard Del Connor is a *"Buddhist Scientist,"* American philosopher, photographer, photo-journalist, journalist, and founder of Shaolin

Records in 1984. Richard is a recording engineer, record producer, studio designer, architect, mastering lab builder-superintendent, draftsman, and journeyman Union Carpenter. Richard is also an author, novelist, poet, editor, publisher and founder of Shaolin Communications book publisher. Richard spent many years as a Mr. Mom after graduating UCLA Motion Picture Program 1988, and home-schooled his daughter for several years. Since 1999 Richard has created over 200 websites and in 2021 began creating Web3 DAOs and NFTs of his paintings, photography, paintings and artworks. www.ShaolinDigital.com

"The Coyote" became *"The Hippy Coyote"* in 2007 after being a test subject for his self-development website, ACTzen.com, that he created for his daughter when she was studying acting. The Hippy Coyote is the founder and leader of *"America's First Buddhist Rock Band"*™ **American Zen**, on the independent record label, shaolinRECORDS.com. American Zen began a Buddhist spiritual journey in 1991 that ended in 2014 after an odyssey of Zen Buddhism, Taoism, Confucianism, Lakota Sioux Shamanism, European Philosophy, Chemistry, Shaolin Kung Fu, Yang Tai Chi Chuan, Meditation, and the founding of three Chinese Kung Fu systems: Shaolin Chi Mantis, Tai Chi Youth, and Buddha Kung Fu. After 20 years of being a full-time Mr. Mom for his two children Richard became the homeless **"Kung Fu Cowboy"** living for six years in his Tacoma truck with his black cat named Bear. The Kung Fu Cowboy became the resurrection of The Hippy Coyote in 2014 with the completion of American Zen's 8-LEVEL Buddhist odyssey ending with the album **LEVEL 8 = Memorial Day Album**.

With the formation of the **AMERICAN ZEN PEACE FOUNDATION** in 2021: it is Richard Del Connor's final plan that his legacy be managed by the American Zen Peace Foundation to recreate an American Zen folk rock band for every decade to mature through the 8-LEVELS of spirituality that will inspire, enlighten and lead each successive generation to pursue PEACE OF MIND and **"End All Wars™."** The characters of American Zen should be recast and reenacted as:

    The Hippy Coyote   lead vocal, flute, penny whistle, harmonica, acoustic guitar, poetry reading

Rory G	tobacco Stratocaster guitar, slide guitar
Tom Calder	Rickenbacker bass, Plush amplifier
Steve Hixon	red drum set, percussion
Don delaVega	recording engineer
Richard Del Connor	record producer

Support American Zen and **"End All Wars™"**
www.AmericanZenPeaceFoundation.org

The Official American Zen folk rock band website portrays the 8 Levels at www.AmericanZen.org

Songs, music videos and podcasts are available at www.CoyoteRadio.TV

Kent State Murder Day book is available in various formats from various outlets and distributors.

The Shaolin Communications PDF book DOWNLOAD with clickable links is available at

Kent State Murder Day

Audible	Audiobook	ISBN:	978-1-57551-256-3
Draft2Digital:	eBook	ISBN:	978-1-57551-257-0
Amazon	Kindle	ASIN:	_____
Amazon	hardcover	ISBN:	978-1-57551-259-4
Amazon	paperback	ISBN:	978-1-57551-260-0
Shaolin Communications	PDF	ISBN:	978-1-57551-261-7
Shaolin Records	Podcast	ISBN:	978-1-57551-262-4

POETRY: Lyrics
Second Edition Release October 31, 2022
8 7 6 5 4 3 2

Kent State Murder Day

For updates and information about this California philosopher poet, visit *www.HippyCoyote.com* and *www.PsychedelicRockOpera.com*

**RICHARD DEL CONNOR 1970
NEWFOUNDLAND IN EXILE**

Table of Contents

Also by Richard Del Connor	v
Table of Contents	x
DEDICATION	xv
CHAPTERS	xvii
ACKNOWLEDGMENTS	xix
Original Show Index	xxi
Kent State Murder Day	**1**
Kent State Murder Day	5
Menudo Man	7
Military Industry	9
Military Industry	11
Politics is Legal Misuses	13
Black Hills Ride	15
Lockdown World	17
Golden Rule is for Murderers	19
Kent State Murder Day	21
Kent State Murder Day	23
Kent State Murder Day	25
Kent State Murder Day	27
Tyrannosaurus Trumpticanus	29
Tyrannosaurus Trumpticanus	31

Letter to the World	33
Richard Del Connor	35
"Philosopher Poet"	35
"Great Salt Lake"	37
by The Hippy Coyote	37
Kent State Murder Day	39
"Kent State Shootings …"	39
Librettos	41
Kent State Murder Day	43
Libretto	43
Richard Del Connor Philosopher Poet	**45**
Richard Del Connor Philosopher Poet	49
Philosopher King	55
Richard Del Connor - Philosopher Poet	57
Performance Checklist	57
Richard Del Connor - Philosopher Poet	59
Performance Checklist	59
Richard Del Connor - Philosopher Poet	61
Performance Checklist	61
Richard Del Connor - Philosopher Poet	63
Performance Checklist	63
Richard Del Connor - Philosopher Poet	65
Performance Checklist	65

Richard Del Connor - Philosopher Poet	67
Performance Checklist	67
Richard Del Connor - Philosopher Poet	69
Performance Checklist	69
Richard Del Connor - Philosopher Poet	71
Performance Checklist	71
Richard Del Connor - Philosopher Poet	73
Performance Checklist	73
Richard Del Connor - Philosopher Poet	75
Performance Checklist	75
Buddha Zhen	75
USA 3 Party System	76
Kung Fu Cowboy & Bear	**77**
American Zen Memorial DAY ALBUM	**101**
War Sucks!	104
Friendly Fire	106
Camp Tehr Ohr	108
Every Breath I Breathe	110
Pictures of Home	112
Memorial Day	114
Bags On Their Heads	116
Bombs From God	118
Buddha Z Buddhist Rapper	**121**

Teenage Hippy - Vietnam War	**145**
American Zen Peace Foundation	**159**
USA 3 Party System	162
USA 3 Party System	163
Music NFTs of American Zen LEVEL 1	164
American Zen	165
Music NFTs of American Zen LEVEL 2	166
What is a Christ Killer?	167
Contact Me	169
We = Me (right now)	170
What Can You Do?	171
ABOUT THE AUTHOR	**173**
Kent State Murder Day	174

Richard Del Connor

DEDICATION

This book is dedicated to that event in American history that should not be forgotten because it shows how the American government has the ability and tendency to turn against and destroy Americans who protest against the wars they create.

Richard Del Connor

CHAPTERS

Chapter 1	Kent State Murder Day	1
Chapter 2	Richard Del Connor Philosopher Poet	45
Chapter 3	Kung Fu Cowboy & Bear	92
Chapter 4	American Zen Memorial Day Album	103
Chapter 5	Buddha Z Buddhist Rapper	123
Chapter 6	Teenage Hippy - Vietnam War	147
Chapter 7	American Zen Peace Foundation	161
About the Author		176

Kent State Murder Day

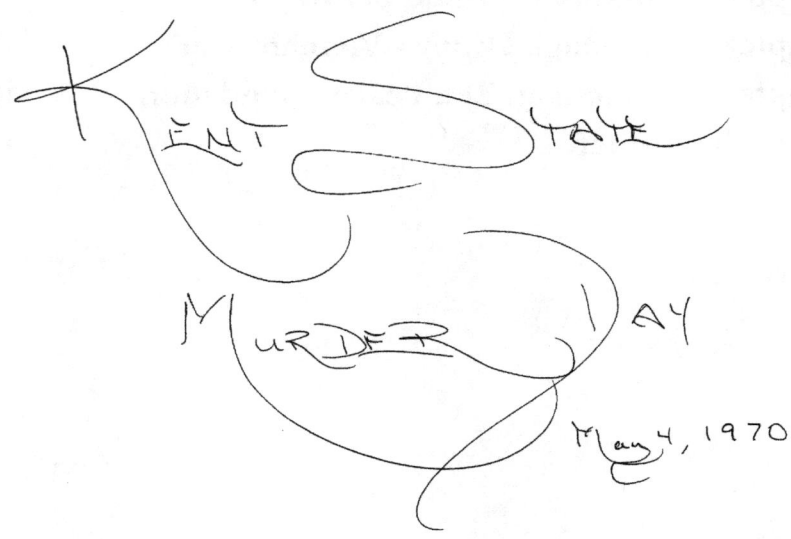

May 4, 1970

One-Man Poetry Performance:
by Richard Del Connor
"Philosopher Poet"

Performed at T.U. Studios, North Hollywood, California
May 4, 2019

ACKNOWLEDGMENTS

I was given the "Featured Poet" honor to perform at the T.U. Studios Theater in North Hollywood on May 4, 2019.

I was performing in those years from 2016 to 2019 as **"Richard Del Connor Philosopher Poet."**

Shortly after receiving this poetry gig I realized this was the date of the **"Kent State Massacre,"** also called, **"The Kent State Shootings."**

I instantly decided that this would be the theme of my poetry performance that day. I named my event, **"Kent State Murder Day."** I already had a bunch of poems written during those recent months that would be appropriate for this anti-war theme. I wrote a couple fresh poems of this theme between getting booked and performing on May 4, 2019.

Since this was four years ago, I have many more anti-war poems that I could include. I might even write a poem or two before I publish this book also titled, **Kent State Murder Day.**

So this book will be divided into several chapters.

CHAPTER 1 will be all the original poems I performed on May 4, 2018. On the left side pages are the "Libretto" sheets of that "Libretto" pamphlet I sold at the "Kent State Murder Day" poetry reading. On page 42 is the red card stock "Libretto Schedule" that was handed out to all the audience if they didn't purchase a "Libretto" pamphlet. I only sold a few of them for $5 or $10. My manager, Oscar Barrera, was selling them. My plan is to auction one of them off each year on May 4, when I perform this show. Unfortunately, this May 4, has become "Star Wars Day." How ironic. Star Wars is supposed to be about opposing the Military Industrial Complex. Instead, Star Wars promotes war, conflict and a large percentage of millennials idolize Darth Vader instead of Luke Skywalker. Sadly, even in the movie, Luke is NOT a Shaolin (I mean Jedi) warrior. Neither is his mentor. Worse yet, Mark Hamill who portrayed Luke Skywalker, became famous as The Joker in a cartoon series. Despite the goals of Star Wars to inspire heroic warriors, it hasn't. And now, Star Wars Day, is overwhelming the anniversary of the "Kent State Massacre." Coincidence?

CHAPTER 2 will be additional poetry from my **"Richard Del Connor Philosopher Poet"** performance years of 2016 to 2019.

CHAPTER 3 will be additional poetry from previous years as a homeless poet when I was trying to launch **"Kung Fu Cowboy Comedian."**

CHAPTER 4 will be poetry and lyrics from my American Zen folk rock band. American Zen was founded by me in 1992 and completed its 8-LEVEL spiritual journey to Nirvana in 2014 with the album of war stories, **LEVEL 8 = Memorial Day Album**.

CHAPTER 5 will be poetry and lyrics I've written since the 2020 Covid-19 lockdown that relate to nonviolence and war.

CHAPTER 6 will be about my teenage years in the 1960s and early 1970s when my draft number was pulled from the ping pong hopper.

CHAPTER 7 will be my ADULT PERSPECTIVES about war as the Ukraine War impacts the entire planet.

CHAPTER 8 will be about my AMERICAN ZEN PEACE FOUNDATION that I founded in 2021 when I was undergoing cancer chemotherapy and cobalt radiation treatments on a daily basis. The mission and slogan of the American Zen Peace Foundation is *"End All Wars™."*

CHAPTER 9 will be my enlightened perspectives as a philosopher seeking to enlighten humankind.

CHAPTER 10 will be ways for people to live better lives and want others to live happy — not die.

Original Show Index

Chapter 1   Kent State Murder Day
   Libretto Title Page
   Author: Richard Del Connor
   Explanation: "Kent State Shootings"
   Poem: Menudo Man
   Poem: Military Industry
   Poem: Politics is Legal Misuses
   Flute Song: "Black Hills Ride"
   Poem: Lockdown World
   Poem: Golden Rule is for Murderers
   Poem: Kent State Murder Day
   Poem: Tyrannosaurus Trumpticanus
   Letter: Richard proclaims…
   Websites: *ShaolinCommunications.com*
                  ShaolinInteractive.com
                  ShaolinRecords.com
   Flute Song: "Great Salt Lake"
   Bibliography: Other Sources of Information

1
KENT STATE MURDER DAY

May 4, 1970

One-Man Poetry Performance:
   by Richard Del Connor
       "Philosopher Poet"

      Performed at T.U. Studios, North Hollywood, California
                      May 4, 2019

                            Page 1 of 20

Richard Del Connor

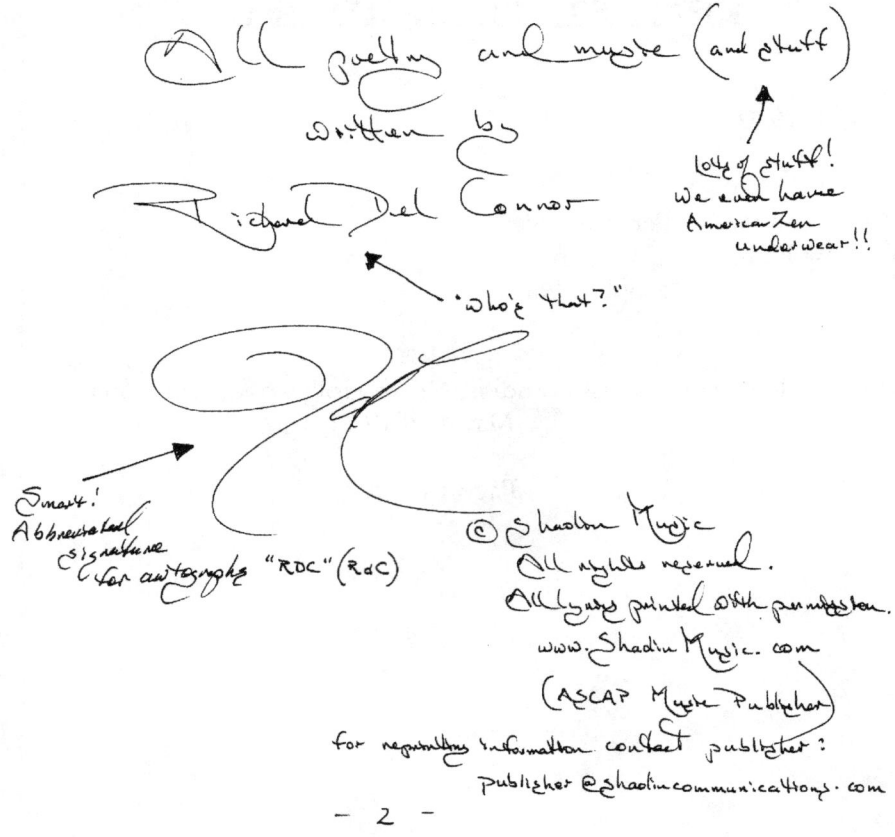

All poetry and music (and stuff)
written by
Richard Del Connor

"Who's that?"

Smart! Abbreviated signature (for autographs) "RDC" (RdC)

lots of stuff! We even have American Zen underwear!!

© Shaolin Music
All rights reserved.
All lyrics printed with permission.
www.ShaolinMusic.com
(ASCAP Music Publisher)
for reprinting information contact publisher:
publisher@shaolincommunications.com

Kent State Murder Day

All poetry and music (and stuff)
     written by
Richard Del Connor

"Who's that?"

RDC

Smart!
Abbreviated
     signature
          for autographs "RDC" (RdC)

                    © Shaolin Music
                    All rights reserved.
                    All lyrics printed with permission.
                    www.ShaolinMusic.com
                    (ASCAP Music Publisher)

          for reprinting information contact publisher:

publisher@shaolincommunications.com

KENT STATE MURDER DAY

One-man poetry performance: Richard Del Connor
(20-minute show)   ("Philosopher Poet")

POEMS by Richard Del Connor

Menudo Man	About President Trump
Military Industry	Who runs America?
Politics is Legal Bribery	Less attorneys in Congress?

SOLO FLUTE SONG: "Black Hills Ride," by RDC

Golden Rule is for Murderers	Jesus said it backwards.
Kent State Murder Day	May 4, 1970 dedication.
Lockdown World	Women live in fear every day.
Tyrannosaurus Trumplicanus	About President Trump

SOLO FLUTE: "Great Salt Lake" by RDC

WIKIPEDIA: Kent State shootings

The Kent State shootings, also known as the May 4 massacre or the Kent State massacre, were the shootings on May 4, 1970, of unarmed college students by members of the Ohio National Guard at Kent State University in Kent, Ohio, during a mass protest against the bombing of Cambodia by United States military forces. Twenty-eight guardsmen fired approximately 67 rounds over a period of 13 seconds, killing four students and wounding nine others, one of whom suffered permanent paralysis.

Summary:

The resulting U.S.A. campus strikes were composed of 4 million students resulting in the closure of 450 U.S.A. schools. 30 ROTC buildings were destroyed. Protests continued at over 700 campuses in America. Unfortunately, President Nixon said the "silent majority" were the only voices he was listening to. Some middle class encouraged more shootings of students. Have we learned anything about bombing other people? …shooting Americans?

Kent State Murder Day

One-man poetry performance: Richard Del Connor
    (20-minute show)   ("Philosopher Poet")
POEMS by Richard Del Connor
    Menudo Man   About President Trump
    Military Industry   Who runs America?
    Politics is Legal Misuses   Less attorneys' in Congress?
    "Black Hills Ride"   SOLO FLUTE SONG by RDC
    Lockdown World   Women live in fear every day.
    Golden Rule is for Murderers Jesus said it backwards.
    Kent State Murder Day   May 4, 1970 dedication
    Tyrannosaurus Trumpticanus About President Trump
    "Great Salt Lake"   SOLO FLUTE SONG by RDC

WIKIPEDIA: Kent State Shootings.
    https://en.wikipedia.org/wiki/Kent_State_shootings

    The Kent State shootings, also known as the May 4 Massacre or the Kent State Massacre, were the shootings on May 4, 1970, of unarmed college students by member of the Ohio National Guard at Kent State University in Kent, Ohio, during a mass protest against the bombing of Cambodia by United States military forces. Twenty-eight guardsmen fired approximately 67 rounds over a period of 13 seconds, killing four students and wounding nine others, one of whom suffered permanent paralysis.

    SUMMARY:
    The resulting U.S.A. campus strikes were composed of 4 million students resulting in the closure of 450 U.S.A. schools. 30 ROTC buildings were destroyed. Protests continued at over 700 campuses in America.
    Unfortunately, President Nixon said the "silent majority" were the only voices he was listening to. Some middle class encouraged more shootings of students. Have we learned anything about bombing other people? Shooting Americans is permissible.

Menudo Man

by Richard Del Connor

Menudo Man, he thinks with his gut.
It's bigger than most - so he must be smart.
Good thing he doesn't think with his butt.
I'd rather hear him burp --
   than politically fart.

(Poem inspired by President Trump, stating he was smarter because he used his "gut" to make decisions.)

Menudo Man
by Richard Del Connor

Menudo Man, he thinks with his gut.
It's bigger than most — so he must be smart.
Good thing he doesn't think with his butt.
I'd rather hear him burp—
    than politically fart.

(Poem inspired by President Trump stating he was
    smarter because he used his "gut" to make decisions.)

Military Industry

by Richard Del Connor

I heard Joe Rogan say,
"War makes people do terrible things."
Then suddenly I realized yesterday
that's why we need war -- and an uprising.

If the embers of war
were ever to smoulder and become cold--
why would we want to spend $70 trillion dollars a year more
of our taxes... without a war being cold?

No. We'd have to send our troops home,
and start hiring soldiers less and less.
Without a battle for tanks to roam
even stealth bombers would become useless.

Military Industry
by Richard Del Connor

I heard Joe Rogen say,
    "War makes people do terrible things."
Then suddenly I realized yesterday
    that's why we need war — and an uprising.

If the embers of war
    were ever to smolder and become cold—
Why would we want to spend $40 trillion dollars a year more
    of our taxes ... without a war being sold?

No. We'd have to send our troops home,
    and start hiring soldiers less and less.
Without a battle for tanks to roam
    even stealth bombers would become useless.

page 2 of 2

Military Industry

People would be less inclined
 to keep buying nuclear Harriers
    and aircraft carriers
  if a few pages of paper (the President wants less than four!)
    could be negotiated and signed
   before erected barbed wire and Claymore barriers.

People might get used to peace
 and traveling the world
   without boycotts and bayonettes.
If all wars were allowed to cease
  the new balance of power
    would amortize their regrets:
From all the Wall Street Corporations that do not care
  about our teenagers being killed or maimed --
   over there -- somewhere...

As they add to society more P.T.S.D.
 the true American disorder
    is our MILITARY INDUSTRY.
(The International Military Industry.)

Military Industry

People would be less inclined
    to keep buying nuclear Harriers and aircraft carriers
      if a few pages of paper (the President wants less than four!)
        could be negotiated and signed
          before erected barbed wire and Claymore barriers.

People might get used to peace
    and traveling the world
        without boycotts and bayonets.
If all wars were allowed to cease
    the new balance of power
        would amortize their regrets:
From all the Wall Street Corporations that do not care
    about our teenagers being killed or maimed—
        over there — somewhere ...

As they add to society more PTSD
    the true American disorder
        is our MILITARY INDUSTRY.
(The International Military Industry.)

Politics is Legal Misuses

by Richard Del Connor

Note: Socrates said we should not consider a successful attorney to be a good man. Socrates said a successful attorney just distorts the truth better than other attorneys.

Not since JFK have we voted for a person
who we honestly trusted to improve: the USA and CIA.
Since then we all vote for who will improve or NOT worsen
how much stuff we get to claim each day.

We want more money. We want less taxes.
We want aloe infused jasmine scented tissues.
We want someone to protect us from whoever attacks us.
We want to satisfy our greed -- and other personal issues.

We want to protect what we believe -- no matter what!
That's where politics becomes screwy and deceiving.
As politicians patronize the voters thinking with thought.
They can remain in office for 30 years --
       never replaced... never leaving...

We pay our Senators and Congressmen
     to say what we told them.
They can be 80 years old -- but they protect the voter issues.
The more you pay -- the more they sway;
       they are professional attorney salesmen.
Politics is their court -- it's a deceptive sport
    CREATED for LEGAL MISUSES.

- 7 -

Politics is Legal Misuses
by Richard Del Connor

Note: Socrates said we should not consider a successful attorney to be a good man.
　　　　Socrates said a successful attorney just distorts the truth better than other attorneys.

Not since JFK have we voted for a person
　　　who we honestly trusted to improve: the USA and CIA.
Since then we all vote for who will improve or NOT worsen
　　　how much stuff we get to claim each day.

We want more money. We want less taxes.
　　　We want aloe infused jasmine scented tissues.
We want someone to protect us from whoever attacks us.
　　　We want to satisfy our greed — and other personal issues.

We want to protect what we believe — no matter what!
　　　That's where politics becomes screwy and deceiving.
As politicians patronize the voters thinking with their gut!
　　　They can remain in office for 30 years—
　　　　　never replaced ... never leaving ...

We pay our Senators and Congressmen
　　　to say what we told them.
They can be 80 years old — but they protect the voter issues.
The more you pay — the more they sway;
　　　they are professional attorney salesmen.
Politics is their court — it's a deceptive sport
　　　CREATED for LETAL MISUSES.

Black Hills Ride

by Kung Fu Cowboy

"Song was written imagining myself on my chopper -- cruising through the Black Hills of South Dakota..."

1. CD American Zen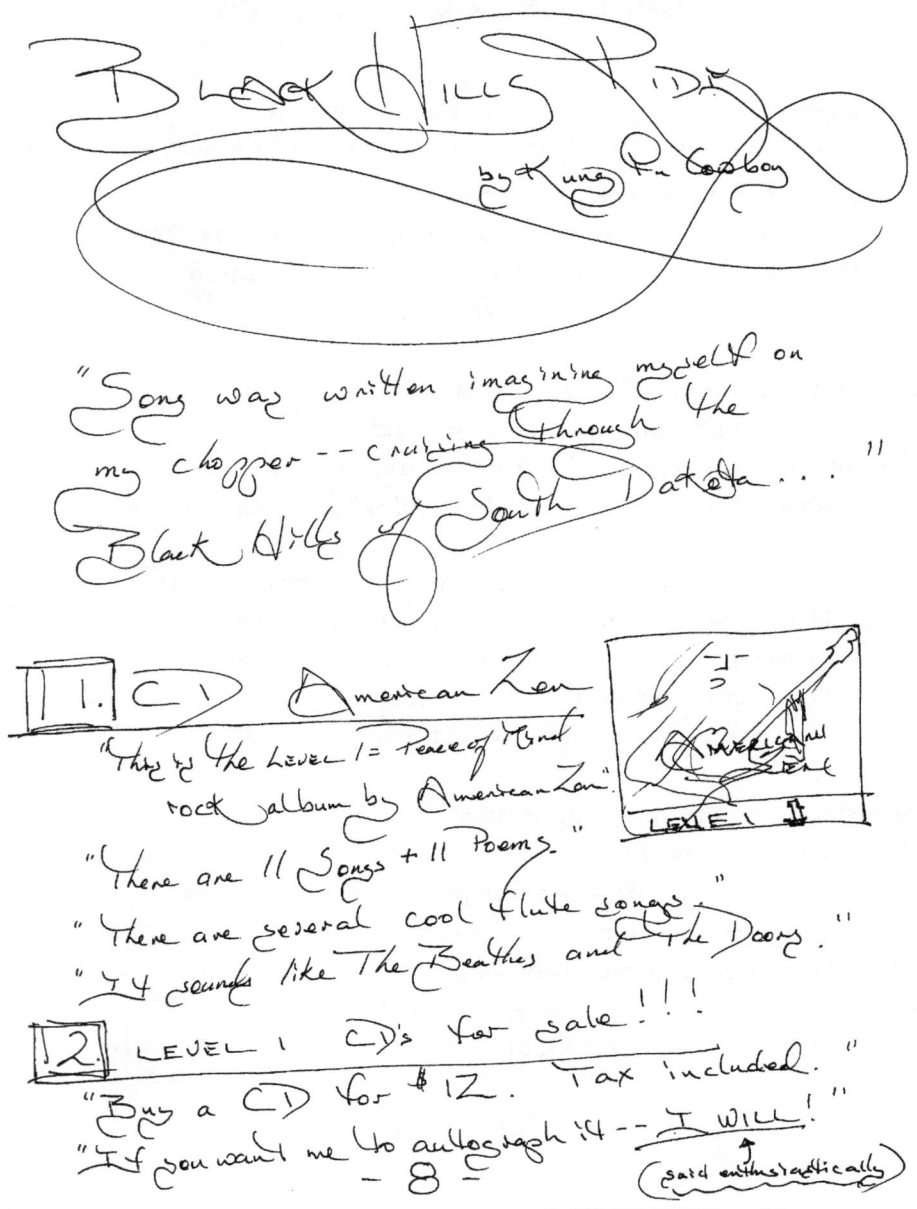
   "This is the Level 1 = Peace of Mind rock album by American Zen."
   "There are 11 Songs + 11 Poems."
   "There are several cool flute songs."
   "It sounds like The Beatles and The Doors."

2. LEVEL 1 CD's for sale!!!
   "Buy a CD for $12. Tax included."
   "If you want me to autograph it -- I WILL!" (said enthusiastically)

Black Hills Ride
by Kung Fu Cowboy

"Song was written imagining myself on
my chopper — cruising through the
Black Hills of South Dakota ..."

1. CD American Zen
    "This is the LEVEL 1 = Peace of Mind
        rock album by American Zen."
    "There are 11 Songs + 11 Poems."
    "There are several cool flute songs."
    "It sounds like The Beatles and The Doors."

2. LEVEL 1 CDs for sale!!!
    "Buy a CD for $12. Tax included."
    "If you want me to autograph it — I WILL !"

                              (said enthusiastically)

Lockdown World
by Richard Del Connor

"We're living our life afraid
  of the world our grandparents made."
So chants the woman at the podium.
She bussed a hundred schoolkids
  so the adults would listen to what she told them.

"WE WANT A LOCKDOWN WORLD!"
She says children behind bars are safe and free.
She says she lives in fear every single day,
  but she knows she'll feel better
  if they'd take everyone's gun away.

Perhaps she's right to stop the deaths.
Automobiles are the euthanasia business.
And banning motorcycles for sure will
  stop those guys in rush hour --
  when our cars are standing still.

Note: The final stanza was written prior to the 2019 737 crashes.

Perhaps we'll keep the jet planes.
They don't seem to crash... Haven't heard anyone complain.
But if bicycles and skateboards create too many scrapes and sprains.
Well -- is horse poo a problem? I can smell the methane.

- 9 -

Lockdown World
by Richard Del Connor

"We're living our life afraid
   of the world our grandparents made."

So chants the woman at the podium.
She bussed a hundred school kids
   so the adults would listen to what she told them.

   "WE WANT A LOCKDOWN WORLD!"

She says children behind bars are safe and free.
She says she lives in fear every single day,
   but she knows she'll feel better
   if they'd take everyone's gun away.

Perhaps she's right to stop the deaths.
Automobiles are the euthanasia business.
And banning motorcycles for sure will
   stop those guys in rush hour—
   when our cars are standing still.

[Note: The final stanza was written prior to the 2019 737 crashes.]

Perhaps we'll keep the jet planes.
They don't seem to crash … Haven't heard anyone complain.
But if bicycles and skateboards create too many scrapes and sprains.
Well — is horse poo a problem? I can smell the methane.

GOLDEN RULE IS FOR MURDERERS

by Richard Del Connor

From caring -- to being willing...
   to learn -- to understand.
     Some may go farther in life than me.

Beyond the awareness of curiosity fulfilling
   a mind may see what wasn't planned
     and discover their ability -- for creativity.

Complaining is accusing
   that someone or something is abusing
     your rightful place while living.
Each complaint: exaggerated or delivered with restraint
   creates the need for punishment giving.

Through the pain, suffering and orchestrated demise
   modern men and women believe vengeance is wise.
     The "Golden Rule" is for those you are outliving
       because violence and murder it justifies.

> ORIGINAL GOLDEN RULE: DO **NOT** do unto others...
>   what you **DO NOT** want done to you.

- 10 -

Golden Rule is for Murderers
by Richard Del Connor

From caring — to being willing ...
   to learn — to understand.
      Some may go farther in life than me.

Beyond the awareness of curiosity fulfilling
   a mind may see what wasn't planned
      and discover their ability — for creativity.

Complaining is accusing
   that someone or something is abusing
      you a rightful place while living.
Each complaint: exaggerated or delivered with restraint
   creates the need for punishment giving.

Through the pain, suffering and orchestrated demise
   modern men and women believe vengeance is wise.
      The ***"Golden Rule"*** is for those you are outliving
         because violence and murder it justifies.

[ORIGINAL GOLDEN RULE: DO <u>NOT</u> do unto others ...
      what you <u>DO NOT</u> want done to you.]

KENT STATE MURDER DAY
by Richard Del Connor

I've spent my time on this planet
   avoiding political life.
But as I learned -- despite how I planned it --
   you can be democratically destroyed
      by an ungrateful wife.

So I'm looking now at politics.
I'm watching hours of videos each day.
I realize the well-intentioned bad mannered kids
   are trying blindly to teach each other a better way.

And that really is the basis
   of what's wrong in political attorneys.
They've widened their apathy by living in palatial places;
   like plantation owners who don't dine with their employees.

How did the government evolve
   separated from the majority they serve?
Perhaps because all humans revolve
   around the bank keeping the money --
      they think they deserve.

Kent State Murder Day
by Richard Del Connor

I've spent my time on this planet
　　avoid political life.
But as I learned — despite how I planned it—
　　you can be democratically destroyed
　　　　by an ungrateful wife.

So I'm looking now at politics.
I'm watching hours of videos each day.
I realize the well-intentioned bad mannered kids
　　are trying blindly to teach each other a better way.

And that really is the basis
　　of what's wrong in political attorneys.
They're widened their apathy by living in palatial places;
　　like plantation owners who don't dine with their employees.

How did the government evolve
　　separated from the majority they serve?
Perhaps because all humans revolve
　　around the bank keeping the money—
　　　　and think they deserve.

KENT STATE MURDER DAY

And that's an important word
    lost in our fast food culture and games.
The word "deserve" is absurd
    when young people use it to punish people
        for not properly saying some new socially weaponized names.

Deserve is a punishment?
There's a positive side to consider.
Did you know if you achieve some sort of accomplishment
    you should <u>deserve</u> some applause on Twitter?

Oh. You aren't aware of fortitude like I am?
It's an ingredient of success!
Without more than your initial enthusiasm
    you're just a fickle, frail, millennial mess.

But let's get back to politically living
    that was designed as a way to:
    <u>SOCIETY BE GIVING.</u>
Thomas Jefferson stated it should be a financial loss
    to claim the position and do the job
        of any political boss.

- 12 -

Kent State Murder Day

And that's an important word
    lost in our fast food culture and games.
The word "deserve" is absurd
    when young people use it to punish people
        for not properly saying some new socially weaponized names.

Deserve is a punishment?
There's a positive side to consider.
Did you know if you achieve some sort of accomplishment
    you should <u>deserve</u> some applause on Twitter?

Oh. You aren't aware of fortitude like I am?
It's an ingredient of success!
Without more than your initial enthusiasm
    you're just a fickle, frail, millennial mess.

But let's get back to politically living
    that was designed as a way to:
    <u>SOCIETY BE GIVING</u>.
Thomas Jefferson stated it should be a financial loss
    to claim the position and do the job
        of any political boss.

Kent State Murder Day

The Founding Fathers were very very wrong
   if they believed elections would clean up greedy scum.
They realized voters could be seduced by a song.
A couple were suspicious.
They predicted, "Americans may be too dumb."

They discussed how political liars and cheats
   would sway the votes with fancy words.
But they didn't foresee that where politicians meet
   would become a separate country. (That was too absurd.)

But Washington D.C. and the capitol of every state
   is a Mt. Olympus not built for mobtates.
The cattle forage below on their allocated grass.
Like Nazi Germany -- it appears America woke up too late:
   to close government portals
   that separate them from the middle class.

Like Mitch McConnel who serves the one-percent:
   these politicians of self-interest
   are in complete agreement.
They vote according to the Koch brothers demands
   honoring corporate promises (and their party leader commands)
   for all the money the lobbyists do secretly give them.

Kent State Murder Day

The Founding Fathers were very very wrong
    if they believed elections would clean up greedy scum.
They realized voters could be seduced by a song.
A couple were suspicious.
They predicted, "Americans may be too dumb."

They discussed how political liars and cheats
    would sway the votes with fancy words.
But they didn't foresee that where politicians meet
    would become a separate country. (That was too absurd.)

But Washington D.C. and the capitol of every state
    is a Mt. Olympus not built for mortals.
The cattle forage below on their allocated grass.
Like Nazi Germany — it appears America woke up too late:
    to close government portals
    that separate them from the middle class.

Like Mitch McConnell who serves the one-percent:
    these politicians of self-interest
    are in complete agreement.
They vote according to the Koch brothers demands
    honoring corporate promises (and their party leader commands)
        for all the money the lobbyists did secretly give them.

Kent State Murder Day

$100,000 for a lunch with a steel tycoon...
That home in Tahiti was also given to 'em.
Along with some lectures for a million dollars each...
It is obvious that corruption
   is what our Senators preach.
They only work 5 months worth of days
   because the job of U.S. Senator
   is to vote themselves a raise.
For $174,000 they pay income tax like us.
But with a three billion dollar expense account --
   you won't see them on the bus.

I'm writing this poem for a performance on May 4th.
My friends informed me, "That's Kent State Murder Day."
So I've decided that on this public battlefield
   I will step forth...
   and share with as many people as possible
   how to create a better government
      in a reasonable way.

Kent State Murder Day

$100,000 for a lunch with a steel tycoon …
That home Tahiti was also given to 'em.
Along with some lectures for a million dollars each …
It is obvious that corruption
       is what our Senators preach.

They only work 5 months worth of days
       because the job of U.S. Senator
       is to vote themselves a raise.
For $174,000 they pay income tax like us.
But with a three billion dollar expense account—
       you won't see them on the bus.

I'm writing this poem for a performance on May 4th.
My friends informed me, "That's Kent State Murder Day."
So I've decided that on this public battlefield
       I will step forth …
             and share with as many people as possible
             how to create a better government
                 in a reasonable way.

TYRANNOSAURUS TRUMPTICANUS

by Richard Del Connor

There's a new monster they're discoverin'
  a huge giant big belly reptile;
With deceptively colored, camouflaged skin
  and an insatiable unethical eating style.
When it's fossil belly was examined
  they were surprised to see what was crammed in.
This monster devoured anything in it's reach:
  with huge sharp fangs -- and small little hands
  it even enjoyed retreating to the beach.

Perhaps like a whale it could've set sail
  but it's mouth was perpetually open.
This tyrant king evolved by believing:
  "Those who believe in the truth will always fail."
    as climate change cooled his hands still gropin'...

Until it accidentally -- or excitedly
  stepped upon the Paul Ryan rodent speaking below.
But Trumpticanus was never listening -- even slightly
  as he tweeted insults obvious -- to who he wanted to eat
    with his little claws
      protruding from his slimy scales...
        I'LL LET YOU KNOW?

- 15 -

Tyrannosaurus Trumpticanus
by Richard Del Connor

There's a new monster they're discoverin'
    a huge giant big belly reptile;
With deceptively colored, camouflaged skin,
    and an insatiable unethical eating style.

When its fossil belly was examined
    they were surprised to see what was crammed in.
This monster devoured anything in its reach:
    with huge sharp fangs — and small little hands
        it even enjoyed retreating to the beach.

Perhaps like a whale it could've set sail
    but its' mouth was perpetually open.
This tyrant King evolved by believing:
    "Those who believe in the truth will always fail,"
        as climate change cooled his hands still gropin' ...

Until it accidentally — or excitedly
    stepped upon the Paul Ryan rodent speaking below.
But Trumpticanus was never listening — even slightly
    as he tweeted invitations — to who he wanted to eat
        with his little claws
            protruding from his slimy scales ...
                <u>IN THE SNOW?</u>

TYRANNOSAURUS TRUMPTICANUS

Nope. Trumpticanus wasn't a Darwinian kill.
Somehow he was weathering that Political Polar Ice Age chill.
He was enjoying being the first Titanic Captain.
Eating his supporters and adoring fans trapped in
    the promises of being in his Living Will.

But eventually he was killed by insatiability:
    he ate everything from a donkey to an elephant
    to a blonde gorgeous -- big lipped Damni-goat.

But what killed him was a Mitch McConnel.
    Somehow that prehistoric snapping turtle
        got stuck in his throat.

So Dr. Mulber of the Furry Burglar Insecurities
    examined this distorted chaotic debris.
He commented on the subsequent rise in population,
    "It appears the monster's death --
        enabled a Russian mammal migration."

As all the little Washington reptile raptors
    sweep up the bloated tyrant king mess --
They're all secretly worshipping the failed monster master.
Because they all want to be the next
    TYRANNOSAURUS TRUMPTICANUS.

- 16 -

Tyrannosaurus Trumpticanus

Nope. Trupticanus wasn't a Darwinian kill.
Somehow he was weathering that Political Polar Ice Age chill.
He was enjoying being the first Titanic Captain.
Eating his supporters and adoring fans trapped in
        the promises of being in his Living Will.

But eventually he was killed by insatiability:
        he ate every thing from a donkey to an elephant
                to a sexy blonde gorgeous — big lipped Danni-goat.
But what killed him was a Mitch McConnell.
        Somehow that prehistoric snapping turtle
                got stuck in his throat.

So Dr. Muller of the Furry Burglar Insecurities
        examined this distorted chaotic debris.
He commented on the subsequent rise in population,
        "***It appears the monster's death—***
                enabled a Russian mammal migration."

As all the little Washington reptile raptors
        sweep up the bloated tyrant King mess—
They're all secretly worshipping the failed monster master.
Because they all want to be the next
        TYRANNOSAURUS TRUMPTICANUS.

Letter to the World
from Richard Del Connor

I'm not much of a sentimentalist. I strive to create the future without thinking of the past. Evolving into "The Philosopher Poet" is also a way of thinking that remembers the past as starting points for improvement.

When I do think of the past I have incredible romantic, loving, wonderful memories to pull from. But sometimes horrible events can have a positive effect on the future:

- if we view it from the proper perspectives
- with the best intentions.

I've asked around. America has not learned anything from the murder of the Kent State shootings on May 4, 1970. We've learned nothing. There are several issues being avoided by erasing this event from history. (training teenagers to kill and bombing countries...) Let's start with two issues:
1. The "Silent Majority" is the military industry
2. Americans should stop shooting Americans.

April 2, 2019

Letter to the World
from Richard Del Connor

I'm not much of a sentimentalist. I strive to create the future without thinking of the past. Evolving into "The Philosopher Poet" is also a way of thinking that remembers the past as starting points for improvement.

When I do think of the past I have incredible romantic, loving, wonderful memories to pull from. But sometimes horrible events can have a positive effect on the future:
- if we view it from the proper perspectives
- with the best intentions.

I've asked around. America has not learned anything from the murder of the Kent State shootings on May 4, 1970. We've learned nothing. There are several issues being avoided by erasing this event from history: (training teenagers to kill and bombing countries …)

Let's start with two issues:
1. The "Silent Majority" is the military industry
2. Americans should stop shooting Americans.

Richard Del Connor
April 2, 2019

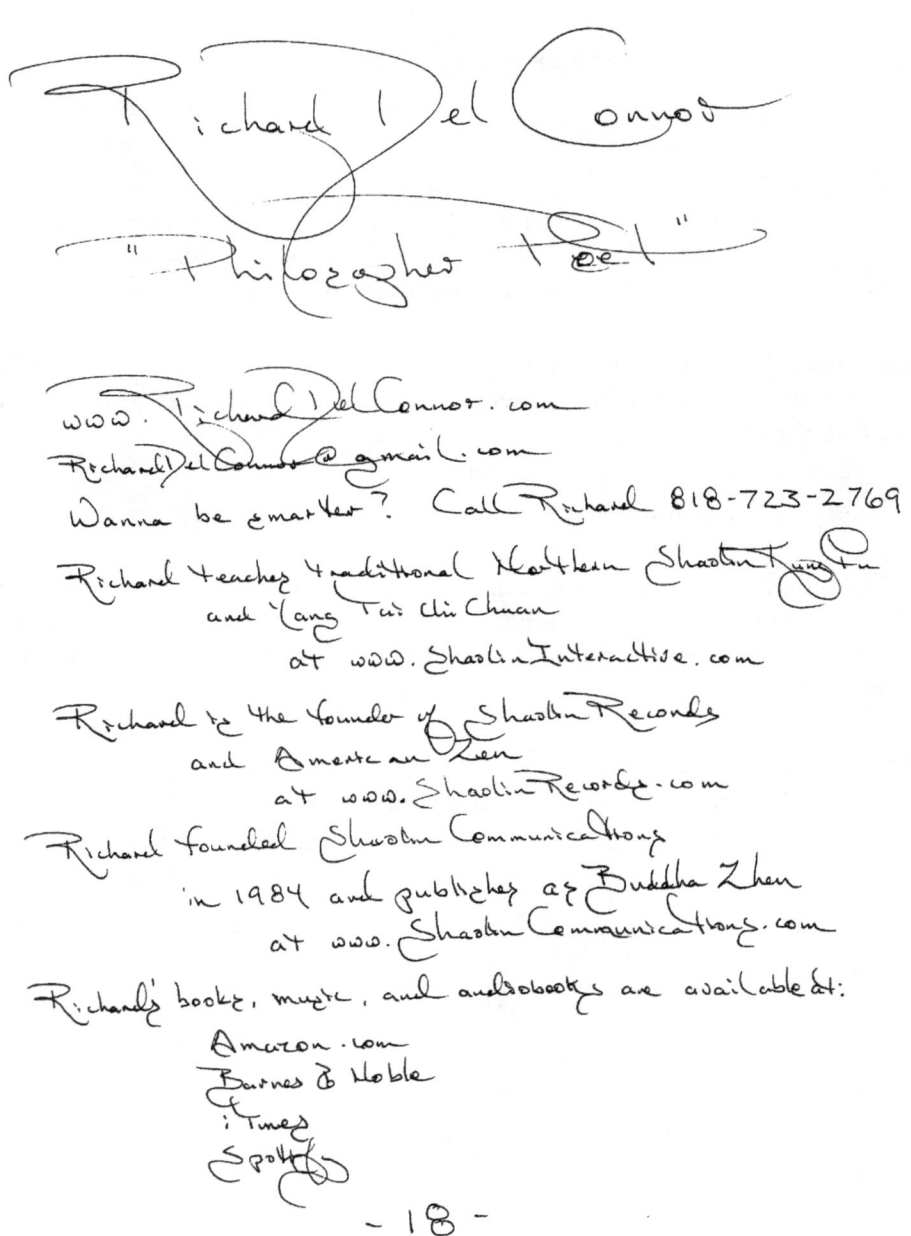

Richard Del Connor

"Philosopher Poet"

www.RichardDelConnor.com
RichardDelConnor@gmail.com
Wanna be smarter? Call Richard 818-723-2769
Richard teaches traditional Northern Shaolin Kung Fu
and Tang Tui Chi Chuan
at www.ShaolinInteractive.com
Richard is the founder of Shaolin Records
and American Zen
at www.ShaolinRecords.com
Richard founded Shaolin Communications
in 1984 and publishes as Buddha Zhen
at www.ShaolinCommunications.com
Richard's books, music, and audiobooks are available at:
Amazon.com
Barnes & Noble
iTunes
Spotify

- 18 -

Richard Del Connor
"Philosopher Poet"

www.RichardDelConnor.com
RichardDelConnor@gmail.com

Wanna be smarter? Call Richard 818-723-2769

Richard teaches traditional Northern Shaolin Kung Fu
       and Yang Tai Chi Chuan
             at *www.ShaolinInteractive.com*

Richard is the founder of Shaolin Records
       and American Zen
             at *www.ShaolinRecords.com*

Richard founded Shaolin Communications
       in 1984 and publishes as Buddha Zhen
             at *www.ShaolinCommunications.com*

Richard's books, music, and audiobooks are available at:
       Amazon .com
       Barnes & Noble
       iTunes
       Spotify

"Great Salt Lake" by The Hippy Coyote

"Great Salt Lake" is an instrumental flute song written in 1993 when Richard Del Connor (then known as Richard O'Connor) was performing clubs and concerts in Salt Lake City, Utah.

Richard was isolated from his musician friends while raising his daughter as a Mr. Mom. Richard formed the rock band, American Zen, in 1992. Several bandmates of the Rich drove to Salt Lake City from Los Angeles to record albums with Richard... but Richard couldn't wait or depend on them any more... so he began playing the drums, playing the bass, recording the Vox organ, and singing while playing acoustic guitar to the songs he wrote of the stories of his life.

"Great Salt Lake" is from the second American Zen album, LEVEL 2 = Christ Killer. After the debut hard rock album, LEVEL 1 = Peace of Mind, the Christ Killer album is folk rock or more accurately, California Folk Rock (recorded in Utah.) American Zen is a series of rock operas.

"Richard O'Connor" was performing the flute song "Bouree" by Jethro Tull as a solo performance song at many gigs he was hired for as a session player. "Great Salt Lake" was written to be Richard's first song he could play as a SOLO FLUTIST.

— 19 —

"Great Salt Lake"
by The Hippy Coyote

"Great Salt Lake" is an instrumental flute song written in 1993 when Richard Del Connor (then known as, Richard O'Connor) was performing clubs and concerts in Salt Lake City, Utah.

Richard was isolated from his musician friends while raising his daughter as a Mr. Mom. Richard formed the rock band, American Zen, in 1992. Several bandmates of The Rich drove to Salt Lake City from Los Angeles to record albums with Richard ... but Richard couldn't wait or depend on them any more ... so he began playing the drums, playing the bass, recording the Vox organ, and singing while playing acoustic guitar to the songs he wrote of the stories of his life.

"Great Salt Lake" is from the second American Zen album, LEVEL 2 = Christ Killer. After the debut hard rock album, LEVEL 1 = Peace of Mind, the Christ Killer album is folk rock or more accurately, California Folk Rock (recorded in Utah). American Zen is a series of rock operas.

"Richard O'Connor" was performing the flute song "Bouree" by Jethro Tull as a solo performance song at many gigs he was hired for as a session player. "Great Salt Lake" was written to be Richard's first song he could play as a SOLO FLUTIST.

Kent State Murder Day
"Kent State Shootings..."

Other Sources of Information:

VIDEO

History Channel > Vietnam War > Kent State Shooting - HISTORY
There are different categories for full understanding.

Ohio History Central.org
This sparse website led to ohiomemory.org
- Search, "Kent State shooting"
  Provides access to various news stories

Wikipedia.org search: "Kent State shooting"
Check out the resources and links.

BOOKS

The Truth About Kent State: A Challenge to the American Conscience. Peter Davies and Board of United Methodist Church ISBN: 0-374-27938-1

13 Seconds: A Look Back at the Kent State Shootings. Philip Caputo. Chamberlain Bros. ISBN: 1-59609-080-4

Four Dead in Ohio: Was There a Conspiracy at Kent State? William Gordon. Northridge Books ISBN: 0-87975-582-2

- 20 -

Kent State Murder Day
"Kent State Shootings ..."

Other sources of information:

VIDEO
History Channel > Vietnam War > Kent State Shooting - History
   THere are different categories for full understanding.

OhioHistoryCentral.org
   This sparse website led to *www.OhioMemory.org*
      ⊙ search, "Kent State Shooting"
         provides access to various news stories
wikipedia.org   search: "Kent State Shooting"
   Check out the resources and links.

BOOKS
The Truth About Kent State: A Challenge to the American Conscience.
   Peter Davies and Board of United Methodist Church
      ISBN: 0-374-27938-1

13 Seconds: A Look Back at the Kent State Shootings.
   Philip Caputo. Chamberlain Bros.
      ISBN: 1-59069-080-4

Four Dead in Ohio: Was There a Conspiracy at Kent State?
   William Gordon. Northridge Books
      ISBN: 0-87975-582-2

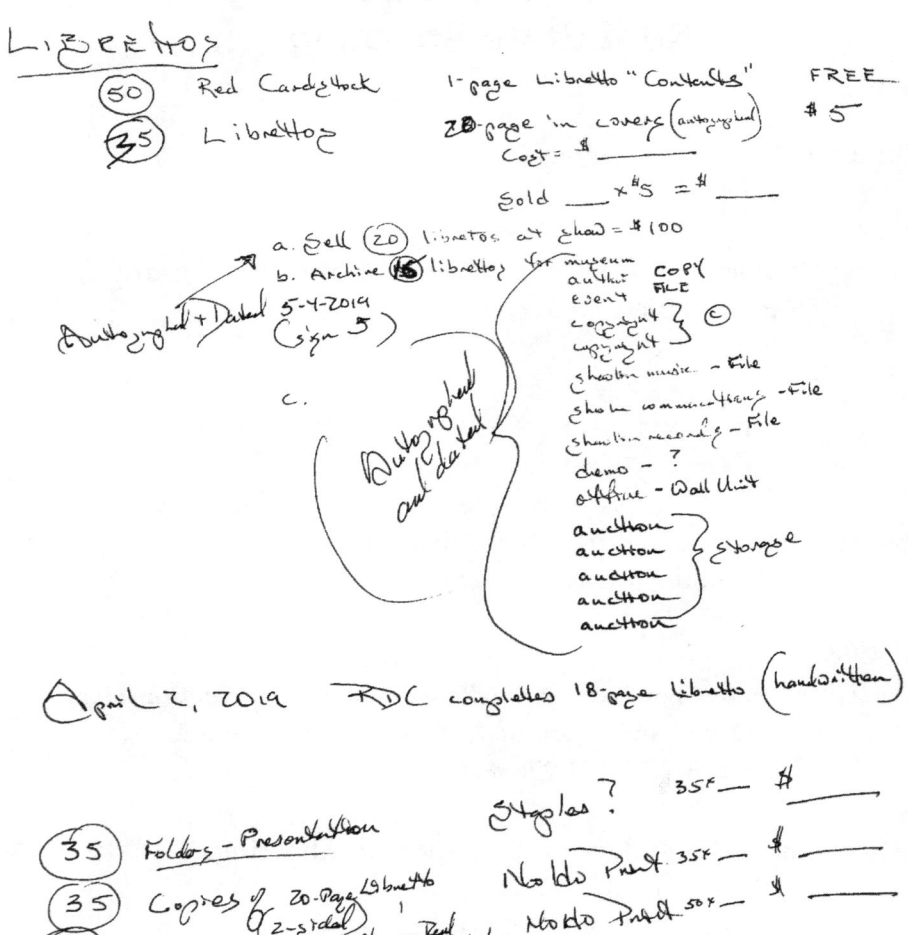

Kent State Murder Day

Librettos

50	Red Cardstock 1-page Libretto "Contents"		FREE
35	Librettos 20-page in covers (autographed)		$5—

                        Cost = $_____
                        Sold ____ x $5 = $____

    a. Sell 30 Librettos at show = $100
        Autographed + Dated 5-4-2019
    b. Archive 15 Librettos for   museum
                                       author   (my copy)
                                       event   File
                                       copyright copy   #1
                                     copyright copy   #2
                                     Shaolin Music   File
                                     Shaolin Communications File
                                     Shaolin Records   File
                                     demo - ?
                                   office - Wall Unit
                                   auction   Storage
                                   auction   Storage
                                   auction   Storage
                                   auction   Storage
                                   auction   Storage

April 2, 2019   RDC completes 18-page Libretto (handwritten)
35 Folders - Presentation   Staples?   35 x ___ $___
35 Copies 20-page Libretto (2-sided)   NoHo Print   35 x ___ $___
50 Libretto "Contents" red card stock NoHo Print   50 x ___ $___

Richard Del Connor

KENT STATE MURDER DAY
LIBRETTO

One-Man Poetry Show

by Richard Del Connor

"Philosopher Poet"
"Shaolin Flute"

LIBRETTO CONTENTS

title page	Kent State Murder Day	page 1
author	Richard Del Connor	page 2
explanation	Wikipedia: "Kent State Shootings"	page 3
poem	Menudo Man	page 4
poem	Military Industry	page 5-6
poem	Politics is Legal Misuses	page 7
flute song	"Black Hills Ride"	page 8
poem	Lockdown World	page 9
poem	Golden Rule is for Murderers	page 10
poem	Kent State Murder Day	page 11-14
poem	Tyrannosaurus Trumpticanus	page 15-16
letter	Richard proclaims...	page 17
websites:	ShaolinCommunications.com	page 18
	ShaolinInteractive.com	
	ShaolinRecords.com	
flute song	"Great Salt Lake"	encore
bibliography	Other Sources of Information	page 20

Kent State Murder Day
Libretto

One-Man Poetry Show
by Richard Del Connor
"Philosopher Poet"
"Shaolin Flute"

Libretto Contents

title page	Kent State Murder Day	page 1
author	Richard Del Connor	page 2
explanation	Wikipedia: "Kent State Shootings"	page 3
poem	Menudo Man	page 4
poem	Military Industry	page 5-6
poem	Politics is Legal Misuses	page 7
flute song	"Black Hills Ride"	page 8
poem	Lockdown World	page 9
poem	Golden Rule is for Murderers	page 10
poem	Kent State Murder Day	page 11-14
poem	Tyrannosaurus Trumpticanus	page 15-16
letter	Richard proclaims …	page 17
websites	ShaolinCommunications.com	page 18
	ShaolinInteractive.com	
	ShaolinRecords.com	
flute song	"Great Salt Lake"	encore
bibliography.	Other Sources of Information	page 20

I have a video of my performance on May 4, 2019, but the lighting is weak, the camera exposure is bad, the video was shot from the audience about 30' or more away with a weak sound recording. The only inspiring aspect of my "Kent State Murder Day" performance is hearing the audience laughter when I'd make jokes and comments. I could have been a professional comedian who doesn't cuss or self-deprecate or humiliate other people. Not an easy task. People like to insult and hurt other people. People enjoy violence, blood, gore, destruction and death.

Since I'm a gentleman and a philosopher, I have a minimum of what makes most comedians successful. But I enjoy making people laugh. My Kung Fu classes always include some chuckles. I enjoy teaching.

I will make some podcasts and read these poems to create a complete set of video podcasts that can be purchased from
www.CoyoteRadio.TV

"Kent State Murder Day"
by Richard Del Connor "Philosopher Poet"

Richard Del Connor Philosopher Poet
before performing at NoHo Theater

2
RICHARD DEL CONNOR
PHILOSOPHER POET

I was homeless from Christmas 2011 to Halloween 2019.

During those years I wrote many books, started a new Yoga System, threw two martial arts tournaments, created on online Kung Fu school, began a career as a comedian, and finally in 2017 decided to become, "Richard Del Connor Philosopher Poet."

This was impeded by colon infection resulting in one surgery that was botched. Then in 2018 I received a surgery to fix the first surgery. Because I was homeless and a senior citizen, I qualified for "Section 8" which would provide a rent subsidy. My Social Security Retirement from working as a Union Carpenter, Union Laborer, Teamster, cashier, recording engineer and Tai Chi Instructor at the YMCA resulted in a $750 per month Social Security check.

I spent the years from 1991 to 2011 working as a full-time Mr. Mom raising my two children, Caitlin Marie O'Connor and Rory Dibden O'Connor. I got room and board without a weekly or monthly allowance from my common-law wife, Michelle Marie McCarty. She was my business partner when we decided to have children together in 1989. In 1994 for she divorced/separated from me stating, "I will never work for you or obey you again." She began dating other men and called our relationship an "open marriage."

We maintained what appeared to be a marriage until 2000 when Michelle became engaged to Federico Maldonado. She found out he was married a year later. He got a divorce over the next couple years. In 2003 they were officially engaged. He got a home for her and my two kids to live in Las Vegas where his Xerox job was transferred to. Michelle also worked for Xerox and was supposed to get reassigned or just be supported by Federico.

In August 2004 we separated our belongings and Michelle packed her bags for Las Vegas. However, the heat was over 110 degrees, as it always is in August and Michelle changed her mind and moved back to the house we shared in Tujunga, California.

I tried to restart our relationship but I couldn't accept being a cuckold and became stressed and unhappy. Through her Xerox insurance I could receive a dozen psychiatrist/psychologist/therapist appointments. So I went to a female therapist who was another version of my mother. She told me to give up on my dreams, quit teaching Kung Fu, stop being a musician, don't be a songwriter ... and, "Get a Job."

I realized my therapist was making me even more frustrated, discontent and unhappy than I was before seeking therapy to recreate my marriage. So I quit therapy and eventually decided that I was happiest being who I was before I'd met Michelle.

However, my kids had quit my Kung Fu classes, quit my homeschooling, quit my music classes, quit performing music onstage with me, quit performing music on cable television shows with me, and quit having me as their father. They decided to follow their mother's example and stay out of my life and stop working with me and stop supporting or helping me.

In the summer of 2005 Michelle said that they were going to take a vote whether I was "the father of my children" or "father of the family" at all. Rory and Caitlin and Michelle all three voted that I had "no authority" and no rules to enforce on any of them. I couldn't make them brush their teeth, go to school, do their homework, stop playing video games or tell them to stop using cuss words and calling me names. "Shove it up your ass daddy," and "Fuck you," were now permissible for all three of them to say to me.

Now I was miserable.

Michelle couldn't spend time with the kids because she was still working full-time for Xerox. She decided to send Rory to live with her father in Georgia. I told Rory I wanted to be his father. He told me, "I want Opa to be my father because he is going to buy me an Xbox." So my years of being a Mr. Mom and father were traded for an Xbox.

Rory lived with his Grandfather for a year. Then without any explanation, Opa got mad at Rory and sent him back to Michelle without any explanation. I still don't know why Rory was abandoned. Rory didn't want me to be his father which he emphasized with, "I'm glad you're not my father," and, "Fuck You."

Caitlin went off to live with her boyfriend, Michelle moved in with a friend near Disneyland, and Rory and I never talked as he played video games all day when I'd visit and play games on his phone when we'd walk to the grocery store.

I discovered Confucianism in 2009 and over the next couple years wrote the 4-book series, HUMAN VALUES FOR SUCCESS IN FAMILY AND BUSINESS. If I had known what is in these books I wouldn't have married Michelle and would have been capable of selecting/recognizing/choosing a wife that could have been a successful marriage for me. I was ignorant. My parents were divorced and miserable without any guidance for me. I learned nothing from either of them.

Book #1
Human Values for Success in Family and Business

Human Values for Success in Family and Business

Book #1 of 4
of the self-development series.
(Year #1 of 4)

by Richard Del Connor "Buddha Zhen"
Author of *Tai Chi Beginner*
Founder of Shaolin Zen and Tai Chi Youth

Shaolin Communications

Each week is a new lesson. Each month is a set of goals. Each of 4-years will develop the reader into a complete gentleman/politician/parent/King. I've been a Stoic since adopting Marcus Aurelius as my father in 1974. I've carried his "Meditations" book wherever I've been until 2020 when I put him on a shelf of my home in Lancaster. I've studied Socrates, Plato, Aristotle, Lao Tzu, Buddha, and Immanuel Kant since them. Philosophy has been my religion since 1970 when I quit being a Catholic.

So in 2017 I became "Richard Del Connor Philosopher Poet" because it was the only career that did not require a financial investment. And I played flute during all my poetry readings and performances. Being homeless this was the one career strategy I could pursue all by myself.

"Richard Del Connor Philosopher Poet"
www.RichardDelConnor.com

Richard Del Connor Philosopher Poet

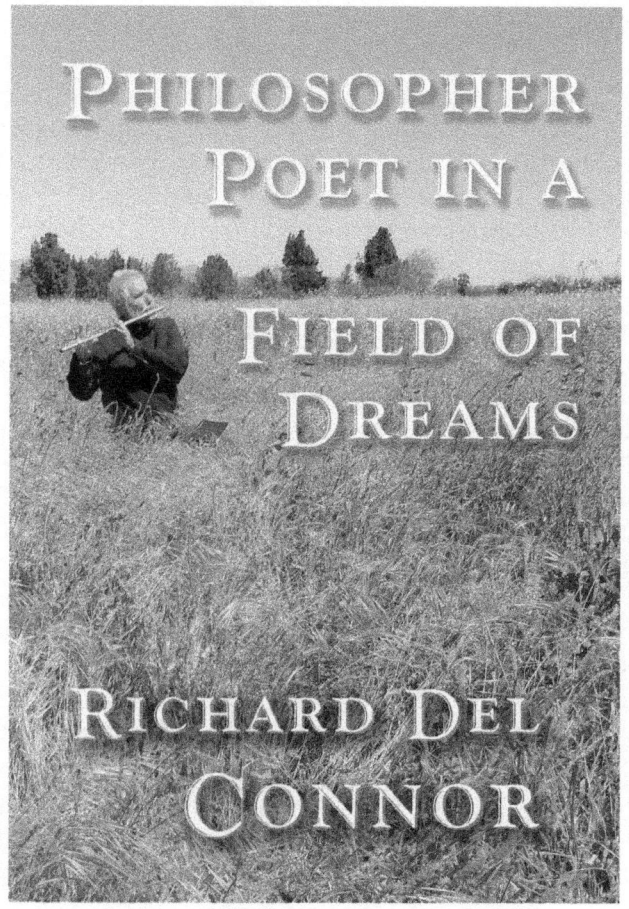

Philosopher Poet in a Field of Dreams
by Richard Del Connor

Book release at NoHo Theater April 2018.

Amazon Paperback
https://www.amazon.com/Philosopher-Poet-Field-Dreams-Studying/dp/1575513617

Shaolin Communications
https://www.ShaolinCOM.com/Products-S/Book-PhilosopherPoetDreams.html

I published the PAPERBACK version of my book, **Philosopher Poet in a Field of Dreams** in 2018. Being homeless that was a major accomplishment for me. I published only one paperback previously in 2015 from the NoHo Library.

I spent the year of 2014 recording an album in my 1996 Toyota Tacoma truck recording my last two albums of American Zen. American Zen was my folk rock group created when I made the mistake of moving to Utah to raise my daughter as a Mr. Mom. I thought I could work from home, be a record producer and achieve fame and fortune while Michelle worked for Xerox and we had health insurance for our family. Michelle promised, "… to make me successful." I believed her.

As mentioned previously, she abandoned her promises to me, ended her commitments to me, stopped her loyalty to me, and denounced her devotion to me in 1994. So instead of becoming successful in two years, I spent the next 20 years pursuing my dreams in the late evenings when everyone was asleep and during the day when the kids were in school.

As I completed the recording of my final two of eight American Zen albums in 2014, I was a Freemason. In 2007 my daughter Caitlin was a Girl Scout. One of our neighbors had a girl in the troop and her father was a high ranking Freemason. He gave me a half dozen books to read about the history of Masonry. Two of the books were written to scandalize and sensationalize on the "evils" of Freemasonry. My Freemason friend Juan Soto, wanted to educate me and familiarize me with both sides of the story. Juan is an exemplary Freemason. Of the hundreds of Freemasons I met, there were only a few others of his exemplary character and compassion.

Check out my book: **Masonic Kung Fu** for more information about my involvement in Freemasonry.

Audiobook at Audible

https://www.amazon.com/Entered-Apprentice-Masonic-Kung-Book/dp/B08P5YX4D5/ Here are books about my life from 2016 to 2018. Check these out so I can skip ahead to 2018 as "Richard Del Connor Philosopher Poet."

NOTE: Click titles below in Ebook and PDF versions for book webpage LINKS.

2016: **7 Days in NoHo — Diary of a Homeless Person**

2017: **Fistula of Fury — Rectal Ruin Phase 1**

2018: **Evolution of a Shaolin Monk — March 2018 to Father's Day**

2018: **12 Laws of Life — To Achieve Your Full Capability**

2018: **Philosopher Poet in a Field of Dreams**

2019: **Kent State Murder Day — May 4, 1970**

2019: **4 Noble Truths Explained — Book 1 of 8: Original Buddhism of India**

2019: **5 Souls of God — Everyone is One of Five**

2019: **Coyote in a Graveyard NoHo — Homeless Shelter Epic Poem Memoir**

www.ShaolinCOM.com/booklist-S.html

Richard Del Connor

Philosopher King

Courage and kindness;
    a gentleman ruler,
        a gentleman King.
Mushrooms of open-mindedness
    make humans cooler
        with practical reasoning.
Curing the mind of blindness
    should've been more—sooner,
        like lyrics of Socrates to sing.
Swimming in the stream of Mindless
    building my mental schooner
        carrying the treasures I bring.

Event DATE: __/__/__   Page 1 of 10

CHECKLIST: "Richard Del Connor -- Philosopher-Poet"

☐ **1.** "Gig Sheet"
    ↑ check when
    "Gig Sheet" is completed.

    Event:
    RDC Show:
    Why RDC?:
    Location:
    Audience:
    Show Purpose:
    Show Goals:
    Expected Attendance: _____   Ticket Prices $ _____
    Event Promotional Pictures/Contacts:

Name: Title:
Business:
Purpose:
Relationship to RDC:
Phone: Email:

Name: Title:
Business:
Purpose:
Relationship to RDC:
Phone: Email:

☐ **2.** "Libretto"
    ↑ check when
    "Libretto" is completed.

    a. FREE "Libretto Contents"
    b. EVENT Theme:
    c. Unique OPPORTUNITIES:
      1.
      2.
      3.
    d. CREATE Philosopher-Poet Show
      1. Event Title:
      2. Performance Concepts:
      3. Goals to achieve with audience
        a.
        b.
        c.
      4. Goals to achieve with PRESS
        a.
        b.
        c.

Richard Del Connor - Philosopher Poet Performance Checklist

What do I do?

Who am I now? After performing this *"Kent State Murder Day"* feature poet show in 2019, I kept performing but was phasing out of live performances before I got *"Section 8"* and was able to move off the street into an apartment in Lancaster, California.

I was performing for mostly the same people at each performance. Almost half of the audience was other poets performing in those two-hour shows. So I wasn't creating the following I desired or finding the publishing connections I needed. I needed a LITERARY AGENT. I still do.

But I love performing. I do. Ever since I was a kid. I stopped getting stage fright in elementary school, if I ever had it. There were a few gigs in the 80s that I would feel some stress. I would get excited, 'Hey, some stage fright!'

This *"Kent State Murder Day"* performance was my last feature poet performance. I started focusing on podcasts. But, working from my car was very limiting. I needed to create "Descriptions" and promote them. I had an iPhone 4 which is very small and it had a short battery life. I had several backup batteries, but I needed to go to the library to charge them.

I was in the NoHo Homeless Shelter from August 2018 to August 2019. I only slept there. There were four of us in one 10' x 10' room and they discouraged bringing computers there because they would get stolen if you sneezed or blinked.

So PLAN 1: was to perform less poetry readings and record poetry performances in the cab of my car. This way more people would see them and perhaps someone somewhere in the world would 'discover me.'

Whenever I'd write a poem, which was almost daily, I'd make a video wherever I was. I'd roll up the windows, put my iPhone 4 in phone clip on my dash to hold it still, and record a poem.

These "HOMELESS POEMS" are mostly on my RICHARD DEL CONNOR YouTube Channel. I made quite a few. But no one cared. No one discovered them. I didn't really promote them. I didn't make "Descriptions" for most of them. So I didn't really give them a chance. I still haven't.

When I moved to Lancaster and got a computer I discovered the Facebook Business Suite. This enables me to select each poetry video and choose a release date. So I 'UNRELEASED THEM' by making them PRIVATE VIDEOS and then chose release dates for them each week for about a year. However, I didn't put the "Descriptions" on them… or perhaps a "CAPTIONS / SUBTITLES" which would have made the poems into keywords … I hoped the YouTube algorithm would notice my consistent postings/publishing of videos and support me … but no. Perhaps when I add "Descriptions?"

Page 2 of 10

Checklist: "Richard Del Connor - Philosopher Poet"

☐ **3.** Event "Marketing Plan"

↖ check box when
"Marketing Plan" is completed.

Product:
Artist:
Author:
Market Genre:
Main Offer:
Reputation:
Brand:
Benefit:
RDC Profit:
Sh. Communications Profit:
Shaolin Records Profit:
Shaolin Pictures Profit:

☐ **4.** Event "Promotion Campaign"

↖ check box when
"Promotion Campaign" is completed.

Venue:
Promo Meeting:
Location Promotion Services:
Advertising Recommendations from Location

☐ **5.** Legal Rights

↖ check box when
ALL "Legal Rights"
are completed and
organized.

©
©
™
™
Author:
Photo Credits:
Publisher:
Editor:
Address: Shaolin Communications, PO Box 632, Verdugo City 91046

Richard Del Connor - Philosopher Poet
Performance Checklist
page 2 of 10

I need a "Philosopher Poet" BRAND. I need marketing. I need help. Even if I can figure it out—I don't want to do it.

I don't want to post Facebook. I don't want to post Twitter. I don't want to post Instagram. I don't want to post Telegram. I don't ...

I'm being honest. I'm not that kind of person. I've seen the kind of people who post every day. I'm not one of them. I don't follow anyone. I don't have time to read people's posts and learn what they ate for supper. I don't care.

I'm gregarious. I'm compassionate. I'm friendly. But I'm not a millennial.

I'm a hippie. As a kid I had a 'pen pal' in Yokohama, Japan. He sent me lots of promo materials. Maybe his dad was rich. Maybe the government was promoting this activity. I think of him once or twice a year. But I lost touch with him when I graduated to Jr. High.

In Jr. High there are "Soshes" which is the nick name of people who are "Sociable." These are the people in the sixties who would have been Facebook addicts. I wasn't a "Jock" either. I didn't want to run around in circles or play with an inflated hunk of leather after school. I wanted to go get stoned.

Actually, I loved playing guitar, but I wanted to stay away from my brothers and mother. I didn't want to go home except for dinner and curfew at 10 pm. I needed better role models. I needed motivated musician friends. I'm surprised I got as far as I did as a teen musician. None of my friends had musical ambitions. I fit into bands. I enjoyed playing in bands. But I didn't know how to be a band leader until I turned 18 and could have rehearsals in MY HOME or MY REHEARSAL ROOM. Then I took control like a military commander. I don't know where that ability came from. I'd never had a manager. Somehow I developed leadership abilities. I'm thinking about it. I can't give credit to anyone as a role model. So I probably could've even been better at it if I'd ever met or had a real business manager or talent manager in my life.

When I moved to Los Angeles in 1978 I noticed that other bands were posting flyers on telephone poles to promote their gigs. So with my competitive spirit I learned how to do rubber cement pasteups and create flyers. I even had a graphic artist, Don Bertolucci, for a while. That was cool. But we didn't get noticed by anyone who could elevate my career in that time. Bad luck? Well, we didn't have a manager. I kept 'hoping' something would happen.

As I look back on my early music career I realize how ripe and ready I was to be a successful productive music artist—if I would have ever been given the chance.

In 1984 I signed up and attended the FIRST *"Music Video"* class ever offered at UCLA. I learned a lot and started working in music videos that year.

/ /   page 3 of 10

CHECKLIST: "Richard Del Connor - Philosopher Poet"

☐ 6. Accounting & Royalties

↑ check box when ALL Accounting is completed.

Business Ownership of Product {
- Shaolin Communications
- Shaolin Records
- Shaolin Pictures
- Shaolin Chi Mantis
- Buddha Kung Fu
- Tai Chi Youth
- Shaolin Music
}

Artist/Author Ownership of Product {
- Richard Del Connor
- The Hippy Coyote
- Kung Fu Cowboy
- Buddha Zhen
- Buddha Z
}

	%	Product	Event %
(Business items above)	100%		100%
(Artist items above)	100%		100%

Consignment:

Sales Booth by Shaolin _____ Staffed by _____ and _____

Money handling at event:

Bank Account for depositing: Wells Fargo #101-1105507 (Sh. Comm.)
PayPal account for payments: paypal@shaolin.com (Sh. Comm.)
Mailing Address: 2816 Honolulu Ave. #632, Verdugo City, CA 91046
Rights administrated by Shaolin Music: publisher@shaolinmusic.com
Royalty and accounting = January + July statements.

☐ Accounting Setup ☐ Accounting Started ☐ #1 event ☐ #2 event ☐ #3 event

Richard Del Connor - Philosopher Poet
Performance Checklist
page 3 of 10

I love being in school. I love to learn. Now that I'm in a home, without children, without lovers, without a job, and don't have to work to pay my rent ... I have a life of my own. My own life. My own world. I'm still in awe. If only I could have worked for myself my entire life instead caring for kids, working carpentry, or working in the movie business.

Actually, I enjoyed working in the movie business making commercials and music videos. Eventually, I could've been discovered because I was meeting people who could discover me. Then I got married to Raquel. What a mistake.

Even though I met Raquel while working for the UCLA Motion Picture Extension Department, we went to marriage counseling and because she didn't like my unusual and irregular hours worked in the movie business—she made me quit. She made me quit the movie business to save our marriage. I had to agree to go back to Union Carpentry which was regular hours without much overtime.

I gave up my movie career for love. That is how romantic I am. That is how stupid I am. That is how badly I was advised. That proves that no one in my life or in my world was able or capable of giving me the good advice to, "Not give up my dreams." "Not give up my movie career ambitions." "Not sacrifice all the connections and experience and education I'd achieved ... just to make a girl happy."

NO ONE gave me good advice. I gave up my dreams to get divorced a year later and try to start over without my jobs and connections I'd developed in the movie business.

So in 1988 with Raquel out of my life I decided to put my effort and time into my Shaolin Records independent record label I had launched in 1984. I went to UCLA in 1984 and 1985 to learn how to make music videos to develop my career and Shaolin Records company. I gave up my business for a girl.

So in 1988 and 1989 I filled up my North Hollywood Condo with INTERNS I got from an advertisement I put in the **Music Connection Magazine** in Hollywood. My ad said, "FREE SHAOLIN KUNG FU LESSONS FOR RECORD COMPANY INTERNS." I had a hundred calls.

I created business plans. I worked with the Small Business Administration. Steven Spielberg liked a screenplay of mine. Michael J. Fox wanted to star in my movie, Coyote in a Graveyard. I was recording the soundtrack to that movie and creating a CABLE TV show that I would host and feature other rock bands. Then for the encore of the show I would perform with these bands and develop my career as a HOST, a PRODUCER, a SONGWRITER, a SINGER, and PERFORMER.

Then I met Michelle McCarty. Once again, love would destroy my dreams.

Richard Del Connor

Page 4 of 10

CHECKLIST: "Richard Del Connor – Philosopher Poet"

← CHECK box when "Thank you's" and correspondence is completed for THIS EVENT.

☐ **7. CORRESPONDENCE SHEETS**

all events:
1. Shadow Communications — Publisher — Keep updated
2. Oscar Barrera — RDC manager — Keep updated

one per event:
3. Event "Connection" — RDC network — Be "Thankful"
4. Event "Coordinator" — booked — booking info
5. Event "Idea" — RDC network — stage man
6. Event "Sales" — supply them books — sell RDC books
7. Event "Other Performer" — RDC network — be supportive

all events:
8. RDC Journalist 1 — LA Times — build reputation RDC
9. RDC Journalist 2 — LA Times — build reputation RDC
10. RDC Journalist 3 — ———
11. RDC Journalist 4 — ———
12. RDC Literary Agent — Sell rights RDC movies...

Richard Del Connor - Philosopher Poet
Performance Checklist
page 4 of 10

Correspondence was impossible in 1992. Long distance phone calls could cost hundreds of dollars per month for what is now just a low monthly phone rate. I pay $14 for a phone line, and until recently only paid $19 per month for internet. A year ago I had to upgrade my internet so I could upload videos faster to my Dropbox storage and YouTube channels. So now I'm paying about $75 per month. But there wasn't an internet in 1992.

I had moved to Utah and every call to Los Angeles was more than I could afford. $10 to $25 per call. I had no movie jobs. I had no photography clients. I couldn't even work in the Carpenter's Union because Utah is a "RIGHT TO WORK FOR LESS" state. The Republicans don't want to pay health benefits, retirement benefits or more than $15 per hour when I was making $24 per hour in Los Angeles with health benefits. The Salt Lake City Carpenter's Union told me they didn't have enough Union work for the people who were already living in Utah. Us immigrants from California were disliked and discouraged from joining their Union Local Offices. But I was a Mr. Mom and Michelle was working for Xerox, and we couldn't afford daycare and I'd told Michelle that I didn't want to have kids that were raised by teenagers I didn't even know.

So I started teaching Kung Fu and Tai Chi Chuan. I could do this from my home that first winter. I could teach in the park in spring, summer, fall, and bring my daughter Caitlin to class. I got a job at a YWCA for a couple years and Michelle would pick Caitlin up after her work day ended and I could teach night classes there after the afternoon classes I brought her to. Caitlin was too young to attend classes. I have a few pictures of her running around the gymnasium or riding me like a horse when I led the class in pushups.

Because I was teaching Buddhism, the local newspapers were FORCED to ban me. Even the Mormons in my classes had to remove themselves from the class while pictures were being taken so they wouldn't get in trouble from the Mormon Bishops.

I tried creating a rock band for the first few years, but once again, the Mormons would tell my guitarist or drummer to, "Stop working with the California Hippy Long-hair Buddhist."

I struggled for a couple years. Then Michelle dumped me.

I'd once again lost everything I had to be with someone I loved.

Love doesn't last. I've been in love many times. Where did it go?

Checklist: Featured Poet Event Marketing Plan

page 5 of 10

Event (Title):

Location: Date: Time:

Philosopher Poet Show Title:
    Theme:
    Description:
    Requirements:
    Props:
    Wardrobe:
    Show Contents
1.
2.
3.
4.
5.
6.
7.
8.

How did RDC get this gig:
Audience at this event:
Show Purpose:
Show Goals:
Expected Attendance: _____   Ticket Price: $_____   Actual Attendance: _____

Event Promotional tie-ins:
a. _____ tie-in _____ Phone: _____
b. _____ tie-in _____ Phone: _____
c. _____ tie-in _____ Phone: _____
d. _____ tie-in _____ Phone: _____
e. _____ tie-in _____ Phone: _____

Richard Del Connor - Philosopher Poet
Performance Checklist
page 5 of 10

So my Shaolin Chi Mantis school was founded in 1992. Despite the Mormon bans and backstabbing, I was the only Shaolin Kung Fu master in Utah. There was one other, Master Lu, but he wasn't teaching much anymore. He had imported a bunch of acupuncturists from China. He was making more money off them. His kids were grown up and they taught classes by osmosis. They would practice a Tai Chi Form that took over 40-minutes to practice one single time. Students would join the class and after a year or two they would be able to synchronize their movements. That was the school curriculum

There was one other Chinese Kung Fu school in Salt Lake City. A Southern Style Kung Fu school. He told me, "Tai Chi is for seniors." He knew a half dozen Kung Fu dances and a half dozen Kung Fu weapons. He made his students spar like a Karate class. That was his curriculum. His students got into legal problems from bar fights and drug arrests. I only recommended his school to a couple people. These were students I didn't want in my school.

After a couple years I had a SHAOLIN CHI MANTIS DEMO TEAM. We were awesome. We performed State Fairs, Government Events, the annual Asian Festival, and Karate tournaments. I was respected by the Karate masters.

I'm still not sure how I could leverage this local success for international fame. I had my name in the Utah Movie Registry as a "STUNT CHOREOGRAPHER" but there was never a movie that filmed in Utah that didn't have a Stunt Choreographer before they came here. So I didn't get any jobs in movies.

Well, actually I got a few. One of my neighbors was a casting agent for commercials. I'd already been approached by a couple agents, but they told me I would have to become a registered Mormon before they could give me any jobs.

My neighbor was a brunette in her early thirties and locked herself out of her house somehow. She recognized me walking home from class and asked me to break a window to let her in. I told her she could throw a rock and break the window without me. So she asked me kick open her door.

I told her that I had once kicked in my own door after I and my roommates had all gone to a movie together and somehow none of had a house key. She said she would give me THREE MOVIE roles as an extra if I would kick her door in. So I did a double-jumping front kick and easily kicked open her front door as her deadbolt ripped out of the inner door jamb.

I worked the TIPS movie, and a couple others and got paid the daily EXTRA or Background Actor fees. I've got some cool stories about working those movies … but my career didn't elevate. Good experience though.

Checklist: Featured Poet Promotional Campaign

Local Newspapers	Reporter Name	Reporter Email	Reporter Interests

Local Radio	ID D.J.	D.J. Email	Station Interests

Local Television	Station ID	Host	Contact Email	Station Interests

Other Local Promos	Our Product	Contact Email	Common Interests

Richard Del Connor - Philosopher Poet
Performance Checklist
page 6 of 10

How do I promote my career, my future, my anything—living in Salt Lake City, Utah with a wife who no longer promotes or encourages me and a daughter I care for 24/7 in 1992, 1993?

I haven't given up, despite my desperate and regretful location and choices in life. I have ambition. What can I do? I'm teaching Kung Fu. I'm still writing songs. I've given up on having a rock band, so I'm performing solo gigs as **THE COYOTE** playing flute, acoustic guitar and singing my songs. My Shaolin Chi Mantis Demo Team is performing events. I'm a local legend. So what.

I'm purchasing **INSIDE KUNG FU** magazines each month then selling them to my students to widen their ambitions and Kung Fu knowledge. I get a wholesale subscription of a dozen or so copies each month and sell most of them to my students at the higher list price. I think I made a few bucks each month profit.

I decide that I need to have a *FEATURE STORY* in **INSIDE KUNG FU MAGAZINE**.

I've got a few black and white photos. I write a feature story about me. Then I ask Michelle if I can put her name on it. That way it's journalism, not advertising. She agrees. I'm not sure if she added anything. To her credit, she is a decent Proofreader, because she does a lot suspense book reading.

The February 1994 issue of **INSIDE KUNG FU** magazine includes a feature story about Shifu Richard O'Connor. On the cover it says, *"Coyote Prowls for Lost Souls."* It focuses a lot on my music career and promotes me as a music artist who does Shaolin Kung Fu. It's a good piece. Well, I wrote it. The only reason this didn't advance my career is because I didn't leverage it. I didn't use this success to tour nationally or internationally. I had a calling card. I had an established reputation now. But I was stuck in Salt Lake City without enough money to travel to the many tournaments that would've elevated my career or perhaps connected me back to the movie business. Even the music career references should have been promoted to record companies ...

So close, but so poor. No agent. No management. No financial backing. No promotion or advertising money. No connections. Being poor has always worked against me.

The INSIDE KUNG FU editor Dave told me, "That is an excellent issue you're in. We call that the 'Dead Master' issue. Everyone else on the cover is dead." They were, Bruce Lee, Brandon Lee, and

Checklist: Featured Post Social Media

Facebook: _____ Purpose: _____
Facebook: _____ Purpose: _____
Facebook: _____ Purpose: _____
Instagram: _____ Purpose: _____
Instagram: _____ Purpose: _____
Twitter: _____ Purpose: _____
Twitter: _____ Purpose: _____
Blog: www. _____ Purpose: _____
Blog: www. _____ Purpose: _____
Patreon: _____ Purpose: _____
Other blog: _____ Purpose: _____
Other blog: _____ Purpose: _____

Posting Plan:

Posting Workflow:

Archiving:
Followings:
Strategy Planning Meetings:

Richard Del Connor - Philosopher Poet
Performance Checklist
page 7 of 10

Okay. I'm old hippie. I had cancer last year. I've got some wrinkles and my hair has turned silver. I'm still the same me. I don't hang out with old people. I don't talk to old people. I haven't aged at all in my mind. My soul is young.

I need to hire someone to handle all my social media. I accept the new world I'm living in, as the world I'm living in. I'm not trying wish for the "good old days," or complain beyond the fact, "I don't want to spend time on Social Media."

I have books to write, edit, publish, AND PROMOTE.

I have songs to write, record, edit, master, publish, publish, upload, AND PROMOTE.

I have albums to package, edit, create graphics for, webpages to sell from, distributors to upload to, AND PROMOTE.

I have a **Shaolin Chi Mantis™ Kung Fu** school to make videos for, edit the videos, upload the videos, create online classes, edit and write the school online pages, enroll students in, communicate with students, supervise the students, AND PROMOTE.

I have a nonprofit 501(c)(3) public charity **TAI CHI YOUTH** to fundraise, manage, create a DAO for, conduct meetings, AND NOW to also: video 800 classes, edit these videos, upload the videos, create the online school, edit each class, supply the reading materials, supervise the students, and maintain the online school LMS Learning Management Software, AND PROMOTE.

I have a third martial art system founded in 2008, **BUDDHA KUNG FU™**, that is more commercial and reasonable for students to graduate from than Shaolin Chi Mantis that needs: videos recorded, videos edited, classes created in an online LMS Learning Management Software system, with belt ranks, graduations, students to supervise, AND PROMOTE.

In 2015 I created the **Shaolin Chinese Yoga™** system for men who don't want to wear spandex and pose more than 10 seconds in any position while also gaining control of their balance, Qigong, and some basic Tai Chi Chuan, which requires me to create another online LMS Learning Management Software system school, with two years of videos to graduate as a student then another two years of videos to teach you how to teach our Shaolin Chinese Yoga™ and launch your own school wherever you are … AND PROMOTE.

I don't have time to spend on social media. I need to hire someone to handle ALL MY SOCIAL MEDIA. Agreed?

Checklist: FEATURED ~~Poet~~ Sales

Event Sales:

Salespersons:	Products:	Sales Booth:	Promo Items:	Inventory - Cash Box:

Online Sales:

Products		Ship Price
www.ShaolinCommunications.com		
www.ShaolinRecords.com		
www.CoyoteRadio.TV		

Outlet Sales:

Products		Ship Price
www.Amazon.com		
www.BarnesandNoble.com		
www.iTunes.com		

Event Inventory:

Products	Person in control	Sales to inventory procedure

Storage of Inventory:

Products	Person in control	Inventory procedures

Travel / Distribution:

Explain	Packing	Loading	Travel-Shipping	Unloading	Unpacking	on Sales Booth
Persons:						
Persons:						

Richard Del Connor - Philosopher Poet
Performance Checklist
page 8 of 10

I need to sell something so that I do not depend on government subsidies. If I miss one month of government subsidy I will be evicted and homeless. Boom. Homeless immediately. Which means I will not be able to keep publishing books, zooming classes, videotaping classes, making podcasts, recording songs, or making albums.

I NEED TO SELL STUFF.
Help me. Please. Somehow.
Buy something. That's a good start.
Promote me. That helps.
Connect me to agents, managers, distributors, producers, marketers, fundraisers, press journalists, interviewers, podcast interviewers, television producers ... anyone who boost my career or raise one of my projects, products or companies to higher level. That means, help me make money.
Lots of people make money. That shouldn't be so difficult.
Is there ANYONE reading this book who can improve/promote/enhance my business or life or career or popularity or sales ...
I'm posting my books at *amazon.com*
www.amazon.com/Richard-Del-Connor/e/B008BXLZLQ

I'm posting my books at iBooks and Barnes & Noble.

I'm making audiobooks to be sold by Audible.

I've got webpages on the internet that can sell my products from secure servers that process credit cards just like Amazon or any other online store.

But despite all my products being on all those digital shelves at all those digital stores ... how do I get people to know they are there, and then want to buy them?
Next year, in 2023, my personal/career goal is to spend money on advertising.
But I don't know what I'm doing or the best ways to do it? Do you know? Do you know someone who does internet marketing? I need help. Help me. Give me a referral. I want to make money and get off Welfare. I want to have financial security and buy a car. I want to own my own home. I want to be Middle Class.

Sorry for sounding desperate. It's because I am desperate. I'm 68 years old making less than $1,000 per month. I need to sell stuff—constantly. I need a career. I need royalties. I need sales. I need students. I've been trying to do it all by myself since 1978. I obviously cannot do it alone.

Page 9 of 10

Checklist: Richard Del Connor — Philosopher Poet

Strategy: RDC "Philosopher Poet"

Phase 1

Phase 2

Phase 3

Richard Del Connor - Philosopher Poet
Performance Checklist
page 9 of 10

STRATEGY 1   Sell books at Amazon .com
This is book #11 being completed, edited, proofread, uploaded to Amazon and being published in Ebook, Paperback, and Hardcover.
In 2023 I want to master Amazon advertising and sell some books.
www.amazon.com/Richard-Del-Connor/e/B008BXLZLQ/

STRATEGY 2   Sell books at iBooks, Barnes & Noble, *ShaolinCOM.com*
After creating the books and publishing them at Amazon I will publish them using Draft2Digital and get them in other online stores.
I will create a webpage for every book at *www.ShaolinCOM.com* where I can sell the PDF download of the book and offer links to the other online stores and distributors.
www.ShaolinCOM.com/booklist-S.html

STRATEGY 3   Create AUDIOBOOKS for my books to sell at AUDIBLE
Audible is an Amazon company but I will promote these audiobooks independently of my Ebooks, paperbacks and hardcover versions.
I have a GREAT RADIO VOICE and will create high quality audiobooks in my closet recording studio now than I am not homeless.

STRATEGY 4   Record/Produce/Release album Scorpion Resurrection
I am a musician, songwriter, singer, guitarist, keyboardist, drummer, bassist, flutist and poet. This is what I LOVE AND ENJOY. I love being a musician.
If I can establish a financial base of $4,000 per month in royalties I can get off of Welfare, buy my own house, buy a car and be a musician.
Then I will be in Heaven.
shaolinrecords.com/RecordStore-R/KungFuCowboy/KFC1-ScorpionRes.html

STRATEGY 5   Produce MUSIC VIDEOS and PODCASTS
I want to make movies, but I will start with podcasts and videos to increase sales of books and music.
Then, with my increased income and VIDEO REPUTATION I can

start making feature films. I have 12 screenplays ready to go right now.

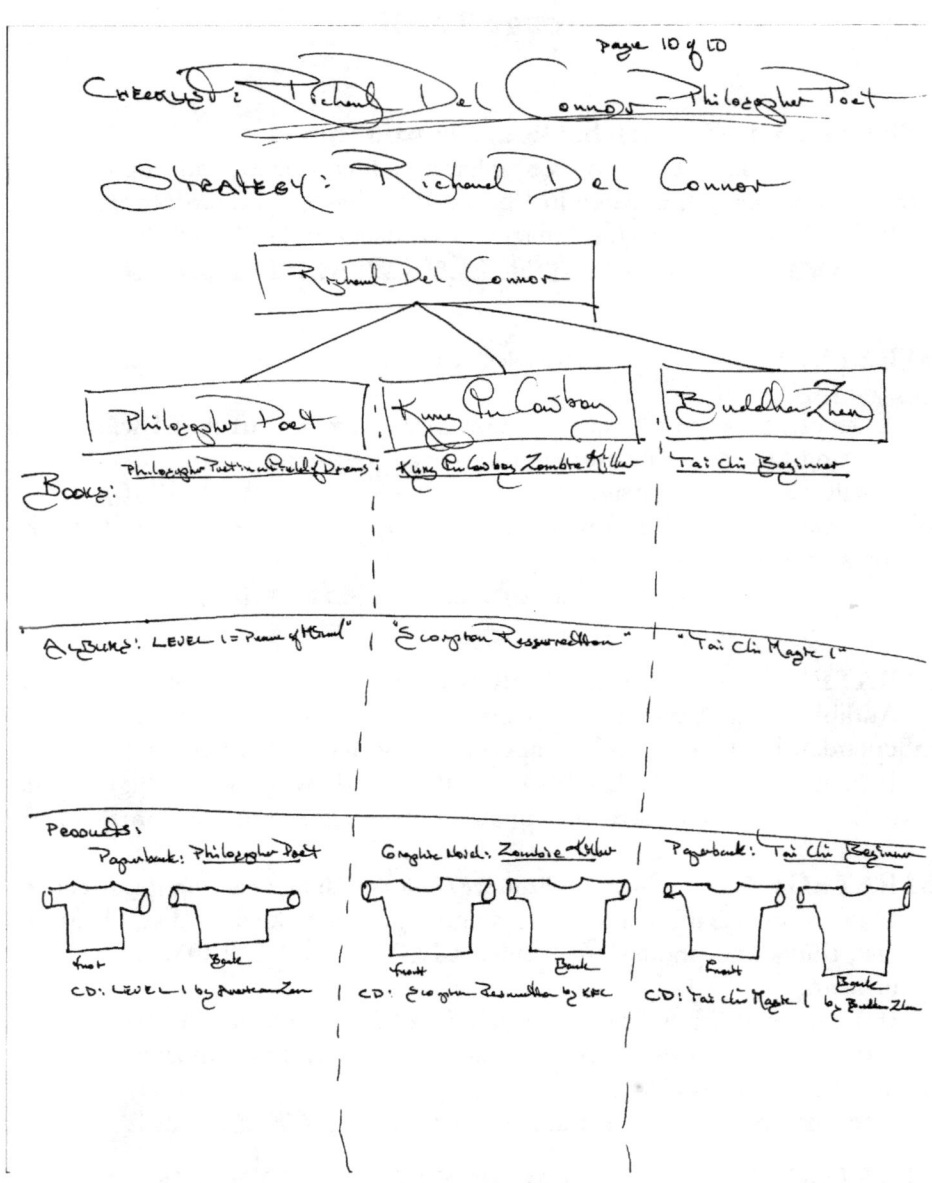

Richard Del Connor - Philosopher Poet Performance Checklist

I am 3 different ARTISTS.
Actually, I'm about a dozen different artists. But these are my main three artist identities.

Richard Del Connor Philosopher Poet

This book, Kent State Murder Day, is me being Richard Del Connor Philosopher Poet. I have about 20 books of poetry to publish.

Richard Del Connor is my legal name. So this is the name I will use to author my novels, screenplays, and anything NOT American Zen. As the record producer of all my acts and projects I am Richard Del Connor. I was "Richard O'Connor" from 1980 to 2007.

www.RichardDelConnor.com

Kung Fu Cowboy

I was "The Hippy Coyote" or "The Coyote" from 1984 to 2014. From now on, as a music artist I am Kung Fu Cowboy.

www.KungFuCowboy.com

Buddha Zhen

Buddha Zhen (Zhen Shen-Lang "Spirit Wolf of Truth") is the Shaolin Kung Fu Master and Zen master who founded **Shaolin Chi Mantis™** in 1992, **Tai Chi Youth™** in 1996, **Buddha Kung Fu™** in 2008, and **Shaolin Chinese Yoga™** in 2015.

Buddha Zhen is also a music artist. I have released one album so far, **Tai Chi Magic 1**, on Shaolin Records. Go get it!

www.TaiChiMagic.com

Can I solve the worlds' problems? Probably. Give me a chance.
This *"USA 3 Party System"* is my solution to **End All Wars™**.

www.AmericanZenPeaceFoundation.org

USA 3 Party System
by Richard Del Connor

Republican, Democrat, Libertarian ... ALL = discontinued.
No membership transfer to any new party.

SKY Party = Space, Infinity, Spirituality
EARTH Party = Resources, Animals, Humanity
WATER Party = Oceans, Fresh Water, Ecology

All headquartered in Washington, DC
5-year terms.　　No re-election. (All branches of executive government.)

People's Referendum:
 If political process = gridlock of 3 months (House or Senate)
  1. Public Debate = One Month = **Month #4**
   a. Political figures interviews: week #1
   b. Public figures interviews: week #2
   c. General public of each party: week #3
   d. Revote: week #4
  2. If Political gridlock still exists = **Month #5**
   a. Political figures debate
   b. Public figures debate
   c. General public of each party debate
   d. Revote: week #4
  3. If Political gridlock still exists = **Month #6**
   a. Political figures debate
   b. Public figures debate
   c. General public of each party debate
   d. PUBLIC VOTES on Political Issue/Bill

3
KUNG FU COWBOY & BEAR

Since I was homeless when I wrote this book, it seems right to acknowledge my cat named, Bear.

Whenever I performed anywhere, parking was a problem. If it was a daytime poetry reading or book fair, I had to find a shady spot that would remain shady until I returned. This made appropriate parking spots very difficult.

Many times I would park in parking garages, but these were illegal to leave pets in. So I would have to close the window between my cab and rear caboose. But this meant I had to move the cat box and food back to on top of my bed.

Most of the time I would park in remote parking garage spots away from stairs so there was less foot traffic by my car. Bear kept a pretty low profile so this fortunately was only a problem a couple times. These hassles were due to parking attendants seeing Bear as I entered and wanting a ticket to park in the garage.

I avoided underground parking garages because these had a lot of exhaust which I didn't want to breathe either.

Sometimes a shady spot would be pleasant at 11 am, but by 1 pm it would be in the direct sunlight. I am impressed and amazed at how I pulled this off for six years. Sometimes this meant having to park more than a block away to find a place in the shade.

My homeless memories are fading fast because I have a new future. Those years of suffering are of no mental benefit to me now. I have lingering paranoia's of eviction and homelessness that I never had before 2011. These will haunt me until I own my own home or have an income that can pay a year's rent in advance.

Bear had a great time with me. Probably had more fun, adventure and love than any other cat in the world. But we both gave up a lot of security and freedom in those years.

Now that we are inside I invite Bear to go outside several times each day. But he only wants to stay out less than half-an-hour.

Richard Del Connor

Kent State Murder Day

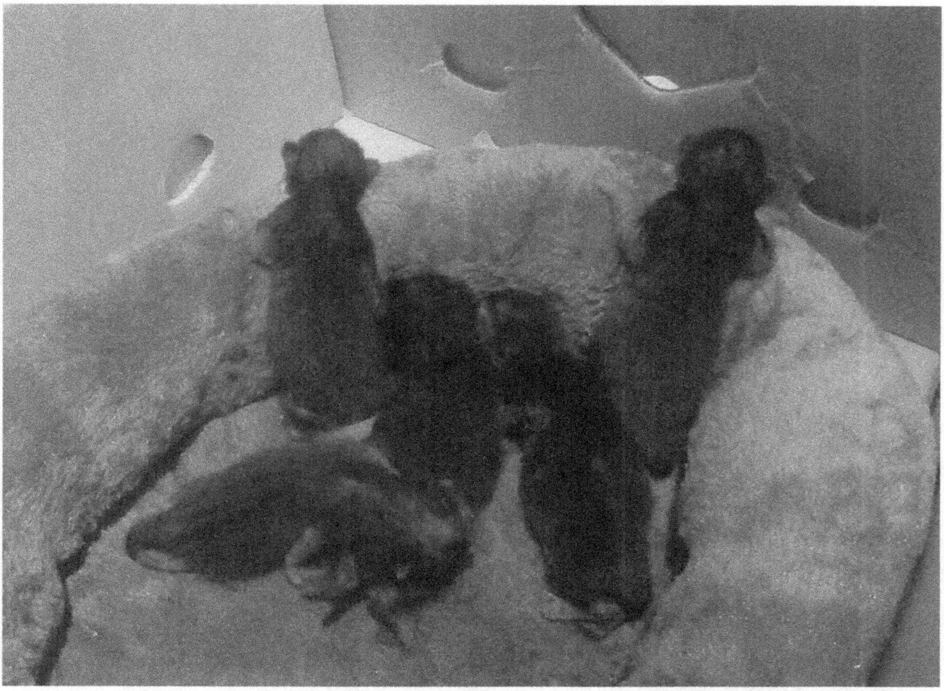

One of these kittens is Bear

Kent State Murder Day

Kent State Murder Day

Kent State Murder Day

Kent State Murder Day

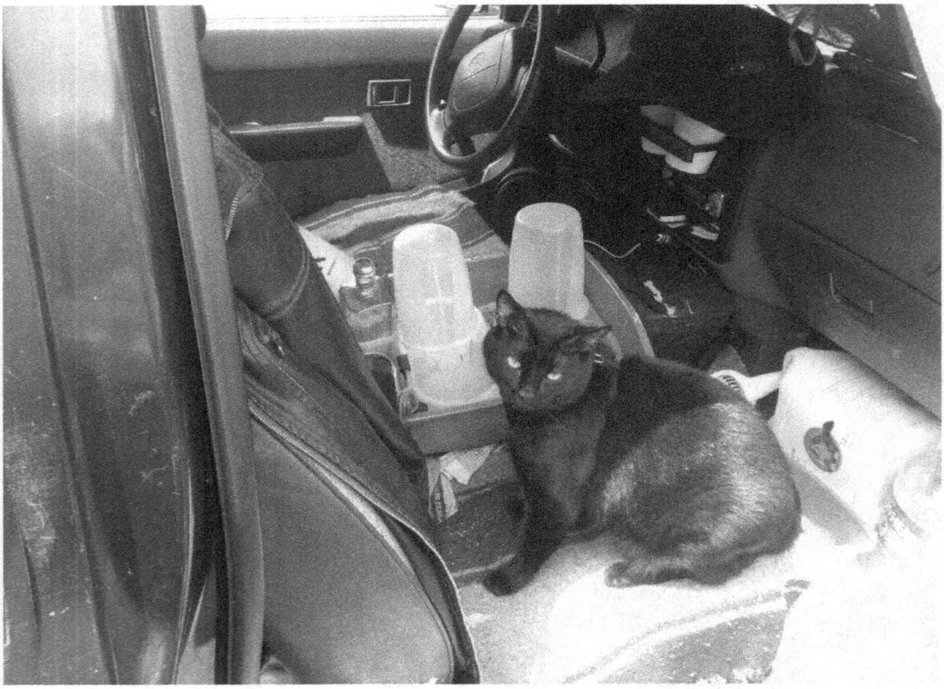

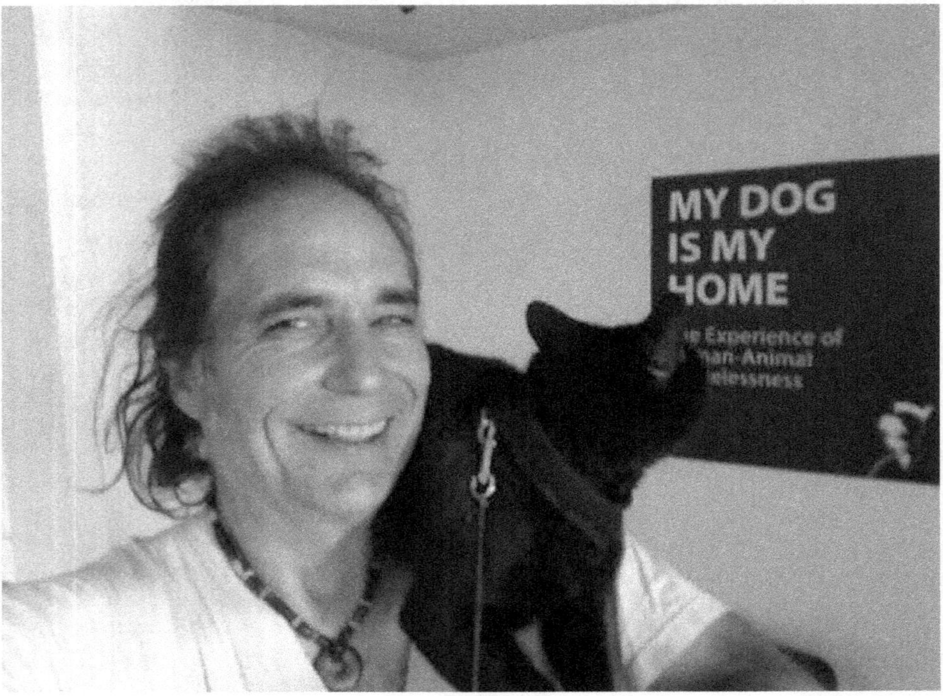
MY DOG
IS MY
HOME

During the first few years, Bear would disappear and take naps in the bushes. No matter how much I called him, he wouldn't return for several hours.

So anytime I planned to only park for a couple hours or had an appointment, I couldn't let him wander freely.

With him crossing streets and being chased by dogs, there were only a few places that I would allow him to roam freely. As you can see in many pictures, even when he was allowed to climb trees I would keep his leash on to prevent him from staying up there for an hour or two.

He was never a dog. Closer than most cats, but not obedient. I used to tell people who were astonished by his obedience that he was actually, "As obedient as an ex-wife."

Having a BLACK cat and living outdoors was especially difficult. He could not be in direct sunlight any day that the temperature was over 70 degrees. His black fur would quickly heat up to where touching him with your bare hand would be scalding. On cold winter days he enjoyed riding on my shoulders and soaking up the sun. Otherwise, my cowboy hat would provide him some shade when he rode on my shoulders. I would hold my left arm horizontal across my chest. This way he could hang over my left shoulder a little, put his paws on my forearm, and comfortable ride along.

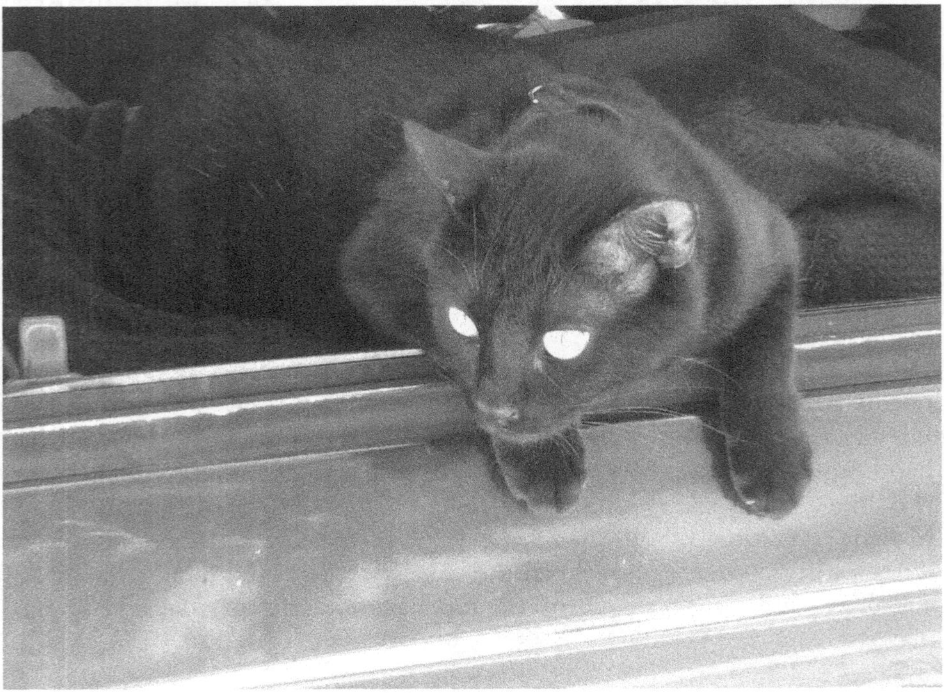

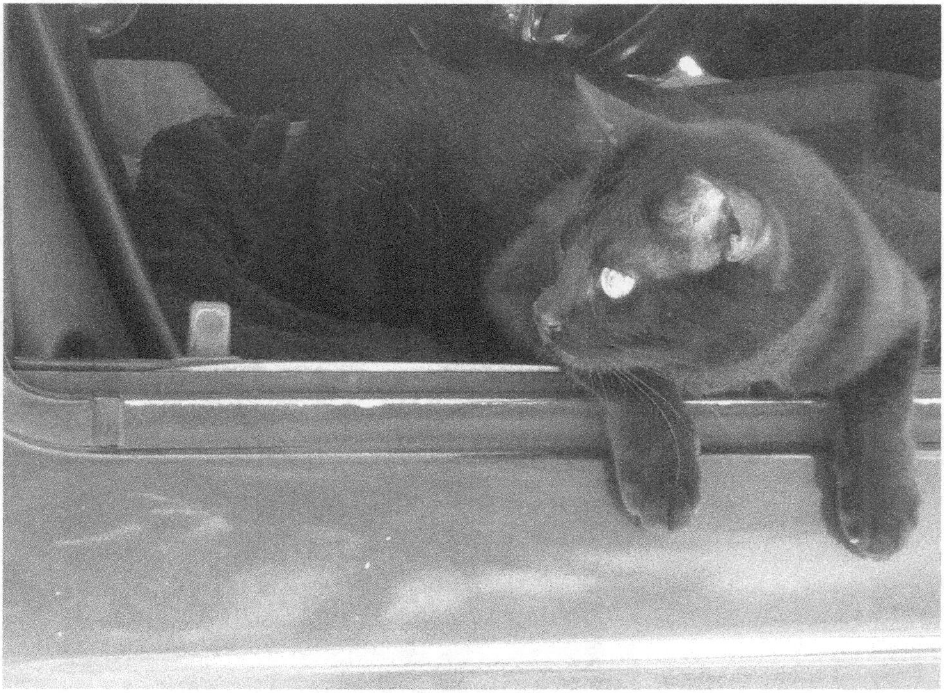

Kent State Murder Day

Kent State Murder Day

Kent State Murder Day

These pictures at a park in Burbank, California were taken during the filming of me reading the book, **"I'm Not Homeless — I'm Domestically Challenged."** When I was going to publish this book last month I realized that it overlapped with the book, **Fistula of Fury.**

Living in my car, I would store my books and poetry in my storage unit 40 miles north. As you could see by my list of books earlier in this book— I'm always writing.

Kent State Murder Day

During my homeless years I tried NOT to write music. Songs are like children. They require nurturing, effort, time, organizing, cataloging and dedication. I was not capable of the time and effort required to nurture my songs into album releases. So I wrote more poetry than lyrics during my homeless years 2011-19.

Richard Del Connor

4
AMERICAN ZEN MEMORIAL DAY ALBUM

SONGLIST:

    War Sucks! (Instrumental)
    Friendly Fire
    Camp Tehr Ohr
    Every Breath I Breathe
    Pictures Of Home
    Memorial Day
    Bags On Their Heads
    Bombs From God
    Father To Son Poem
    War Sucks!

All of these songs written by Richard Del Connor "The Hippy Coyote."
How do you give credit to ghosts?
Inspired by spirits from another dimension?
Actually, they shared images. I saw their memories. I understood them as they felt or expressed their emotions. They seemed very happy with whatever I did.

Ironically, I thought I could redo the vocals better when they were gone.

Kent State Murder Day

But when I tried to record them again, a couple weeks later, I couldn't. So all these vocals were spirit powered. *"War Sucks!"* Was me being me.

This is the **American Zen LEVEL 8** album. In 1991 when I founded the American Zen band and decided the band would be an 8-LEVEL spiritual journey to Nirvana—I didn't know what Nirvana or the spiritual world was.

In 2014 I recorded the **LEVEL 7 = End of the Line** album and released it on July 4, 2014. I had achieved the STOIC LIFESTYLE. I was happily homeless without a materialistic lifestyle. Like Marcus Aurelius living in a tent in the forest, harmonizing with the Homeless Industrial Complex, and appreciating the seasons of Nature with my black cat Bear.

Then, to my surprise, on the eve of Memorial Day 2014 I wrote a poem about a man talking to his soldier son. Not until the end of the poem did I realize that his son was killed in battle. The next morning I woke up with a half a dozen ghosts in my brain telling me their war stories. They wanted me to write poems for them too. I decided these poems were lyrics and wrote them each a song which they helped me sing.

Richard Del Connor

War Sucks!

by The Hippy Coyote
from the album: **Memorial Day Album** by American Zen

Intro:

The government — voted for them
Attorneys control — our Heaven - WAR SUCKS!

They go to work — they spread their lies
They don't care — who lives or dies - WAR SUCKS!

What they hide — is the fruit of their stealth
Always pursuing — undeserved wealth - WAR SUCKS!

```
D                           E
```
Who we choose — is how we lose

```
C           D
```
Our freedoms they control

```
C                   E
```
They made the laws — our ultimate flaws

```
C                              D    E
```
Giving themselves what they actually stole

Send boys to war — like dogs chase a fox
War is a sport — where no one talks - WAR SUCKS!

Crouching in fear — they're shooting at me!
Must I kill them — so I can be free? WAR SUCKS!

Who we choose — is how we lose
Our freedoms they control

Kent State Murder Day

They made the laws — our ultimate flaws
Giving themselves what they actually stole

SOLO VERSE:
SOLO VERSE:
SOLO VERSE:

Who we choose — is how we lose
Our freedoms they control
They made the laws — our ultimate flaws
Giving themselves what they actually stole

Holding hands with the World Bank
Spending our money on a jet or a tank - WAR SUCKS!

We blow up a bridge — burn down a school
Am I their freedom — or am I a fool? WAR SUCKS!

What is the punishment for our congressman?
Responsible for all these dead Americans - WAR SUCKS!

Written 5-26-2014 by Coyote in his Toyota Tacoma covered wagon.

Richard Del Connor

Friendly Fire

by The Hippy Coyote
from the album: **Memorial Day Album** by American Zen

INTRO: F#m - G#m - Bm - C#

Bullets, bombs, machine gun fire
Soldiers scream in pain — napalm fire
Death surrounds you — must fight back
Should you retreat — or attack?
Your gunstock soaks up a tear
You no longer tremble with fear
You didn't know he was hiding there

Your body convulses — you wanna vomit somewhere
But it can't be here — no not now
They're still shooting at you from the trees
Your eyes betray your confusion how
Will you escape? Or tonight freeze?

F#m_____Bm
Can't stop to think of him -- nothing to say

F#m_____Bm
Maybe it was someone else -- he got in the way

F#m_____Bm
It's not my fault -- he stood up in front of me

C#m_____Bm
I was aiming at -- the enemy

SOLO:

C#m - F#m - E - F#

Kent State Murder Day

What do I say? — What do I do?
How do I explain — I shot him through?
From this bad dream — I must wake up
To right this wrong — give back a life
He had a child — he had a wife
Will they hate me? Forever scorn?
Oh God I wish I'd never been born

Can't stop to think of him — nothing to say
Maybe it was someone else — he got in the way
It's not my fault — he stood up in front of me
I was aiming at — the enemy

Written 5-26-2014 by Coyote in his Toyota Tacoma covered wagon.

Richard Del Connor

Camp Tehr Ohr

by The Hippy Coyote
from the album: **Memorial Day Album** by American Zen

Am descent: Am - G - F

Riff:

Desert wind — rustles my tent
Reminding of the bullets spent
It's never quiet — there's never peace
Gotta rest, calm my mind -- get some sleep
Thank about home — I miss them so
Do they think of me? — Do they know?

C_____B
This nightmare I live within
Every day is fear, death, and mortal sin
I shake, I tremble — or relax in a chill
That stiffens my heart — again I must kill

Tomorrow the sun will rise again
Gotta think of something — not about then
When I'll have breakfast with my friends
Hoping we're all still alive when the day ends

I'm writing home — but what do I say?
The truth and tales will ruin their day
Gotta let them know — I'm still alive and well
In Camp Tehr Ohr — one step from Hell

BRIDGE:
The sun burns my eyes — the sand burns my feet
Through the soles of my combat boots
A desert scorpion seeks my shade

Kent State Murder Day

Death is my shadow — in a land of no roots

Nothing grows here — hardly anything there
Why am I here? Why do I care?
The problems of this country — are they really mine?
Am I solving any problems — am I committing a crime?

INTRO:
SOLOS:

Gotta finish my rounds — can't understand what they're say
Gotta stop that barking dog — giving my position away
As I toss a piece of granola bar — the dog comes nearer
Another crumb for the dog — diminishes our mutual fear

Crap! Don't follow me — we're not friends
I just want to keep you quiet — until my patrol ends
If I survive Oh Lord — just get me home please!
I will spend the rest of my life on bended knees

Thankful to you Oh God — please get me home
I don't want to die here — with my friends, this dog — or alone

Written 5-26-2014 by Coyote in his Toyota Tacoma covered wagon.

Richard Del Connor

Every Breath I Breathe

by The Hippy Coyote
from the album: **Memorial Day Album** by American Zen

C Riff

Am - E - Bm
F# - D - C#
Bridge: Bm - C - Am - B
Solo G - C#

I am Lakota — born strong and brave
Proudly I serve and Nobly I save
The lives of my country, my family, my nation
This is my chance to prove my creation

I give thanks for each step I make
I give thanks for each breath I take
Thanks to Great Grandfather— my first bite is given back
In appreciation for all I am given — or that I lack

SOLO:

Because the Creator has placed me here
Along with the blacks, browns, and queer
My job and my duty are the measure of my life
If I survive — I will find a wife

I am a man — a warrior, a saint
I suffer and sweat without a single complaint
Every breath I breathe — I thank God for
Every Breath I breathe — is another chance to score

BRIDGE:
The targets of my future -- I've been assigned
Notches on my gun — I won't fall behind
Protecting my brothers — protecting my friends

Kent State Murder Day

My country, my honor — all I defend

For every man must prove his worth
Facing Death — our very last friend
Justifying all I've been given from this Earth
Thankful and protective to the very, very end

Some may say that war is wrong
They sing their pitiful anti-war song
Let them whine and wail like women crying
They would never survive in this killing and dying

Where Death is a Ghost — watching over me
There is no hurry — there is no plan
A man must earn his right to be free
Only facing death — will a boy become a man

END SOLO

Written 5-26-2014 by Coyote in his Toyota Tacoma covered wagon.

Richard Del Connor

Pictures of Home

by The Hippy Coyote
from the album: **Memorial Day Album** by American Zen

RIFF: Em - Am - Em

Pictures of home — in my duffel bag
One in my wallet — a picture of my wife
And the baby — Christmas I've yet to see
Just two more months until my Christmas reprieve

G_____D
Looking at that photo -- fills me with hope

Am_____G
Looking at these pictures -- not my gun scope

G_____D
Pictures of home fill me with love -- then with dread

Am_____B
Pictures of home remind me -- I'm not dead

The dog, the cat -- I miss my garage
My castle -- amidst this barrage
Of hateful scorns -- and a woman's spit
Yesterday Jimmy Q -- got hit

Of course I'm being careful
I'm coming back to my family
I'm gonna make it
This Christmas you will see me

This is my last letter -- another week, I'll be there
Hugging and kissing and stroking your hair

Kent State Murder Day

Just another week -- be patient -- I love you
Seven more days of war -- and I'll be through

SOLO:

My Christmas present from you -- is a smile
Just look into my face -- talk to me awhile
That is the Heaven I dream and wait for
Please be patient -- just one week more

SOLO: (Em - Am - Em)4

SOLO: (Em - Am - Em)4

Looking at that photo -- fills me with hope
Looking at these pictures -- not my gun scope
Pictures of home fill me with love -- then with dread
-- Reminding me -- I'm not dead

SOLO: (picking staccato) (Em - Am - Em)4

SOLO: (power strums) (Em - Am - Em)4

My present from you -- is a smile
Just look into my face -- talk to me awhile
That is the Heaven I dream and wait for
Please be patient -- just one week more

Pictures of home -- Pictures of home

Written 5-26-2014 by Coyote in his Toyota Tacoma covered wagon.

Richard Del Connor

Memorial Day

by The Hippy Coyote
from the album: **Memorial Day Album** by American Zen

```
A_____F#m_____D_____E
```
Last night I laid in the back of my truck
Imagining our soldiers in tanks, jeeps and tents
In my homelessness — yeah — my life sucks!
But can I complain — thinking of their resentments?

```
Bm____E_____Bm____E_____F#m
```
It's Memorial Day -- It's Memorial Day


```
A_____F#m_____D_____E
```
A chopper flies over — but they don't shoot
No bombs bursting with fear — keeping out of view I scoot
Being discovered by a policeman's badge
Telling me I can't sleep on the street
With only a few dollars to my name
Trying to get a shower every day or two — and a hamburger to eat

It's Memorial Day -- It's Memorial Day
Day of thanks -- for all those -- who gave their lives away

But is this so bad — compared to those
Who are bivouacked in the Middle East or on a boat?
I can choose to go the library and work
I can leave when someone — goes berserk

```
A___F#m__D_____E
```
War sucks! War is stupid - War is a joke
Costing the lives of mostly innocent folk

Kent State Murder Day

No war is necessary - no war is right
No war makes killing people - a righteous fight

Will God be glad we couldn't talk it out
Will God be happy for all those we made sad
Will God reward us for each man or woman killed?
Who gets the credit - the soldier or the congressman on The Hill

If we pay someone, a soldier, to kill someone - are we innocent?
We never touched the gun - But it's all a huge financial conspiracy
Fooling people into believing there is an enemy
We must hurry up and kill - murder and burn
How can this be right? When will people learn?
Killing is not the answer - words accomplish more

It's Memorial Day -- It's Memorial Day
Thankful of those -- who gave their lives away

Written 5-26-2014 by Coyote in his Toyota Tacoma covered wagon.

Richard Del Connor

Bags On Their Heads

by The Hippy Coyote
from the album: **Memorial Day Album** by American Zen

INTRO:

(Am - G - D)4
(C - D - Am)4

I watched the blitzkrieg of Afghanistan
I watched the tanks roll through Kuwait
The bombs bursting in air
Over women and children - My God they must be scared!

The daylight reveals an American dome
The rubble and bones of your neighbor's home
Then we roll through with soldiers, tanks and guns
Like Russia in Czechoslovakia and Hitler in Poland

If it's good for them — it must be good for us
Would our children be safe there now — on a school bus?
When did American become a Patriot Act instead?
Liberty wears a bag on her head

Billboards claim our Marines are protecting us
What a lie! This totally disgusts!
If they are doing anything for me
Then come home all you soldiers -- to your family

Bags on their heads -- interrogate them
Come home -- you're a policeman
You've already killed -- taken a life -- murdered them in their beds
You're ready to protect our children -- with bags on their heads

SOLO:

Kent State Murder Day

Trained to take orders -- kill on command
Do you represent each American?
Every time you shoot to kill
Should every American get a satisfying thrill?

As we play our video war games
Destroying our digital enemies
Learning the desire to kill monsters without names
Are we the solution -- or the disease?

Killing is the only way to win
One or a hundred is not a sin
Whether you win or whether you lose
Guilt is not a feeling you will ever choose

If it's good for them -- it must be good for us
Would our children be safe there now -- on a school bus?
When did America become a Patriot Act instead?
Liberty wears a bag on her head

Written 5-26-2014 by Coyote in his Toyota Tacoma covered wagon.

Richard Del Connor

Bombs From God

by The Hippy Coyote
from the album: **Memorial Day Album** by American Zen

INTRO: A riff

A   C   G
Rain falls from Heaven -- creates new life
Clouds block out the sun -- flying across the sky
Thunder blasts tell us where -- God is stabbing with his knife
Winds will wash away the death -- as tears fall from God's eye

Here I sit with buttons to push
High in the sky in wings of steel
Headphone chatter -- what does matter
Is nothing to feel
"Release the rain. The rain."

INTRO:

A   C   G
My target is certain to cause my enemy pain
Factories, refineries -- destroyed will drain
Their evil economy to stop their progress
Black smoke billows from our success

Like the rain my droplets fall
When they hit the sod I'm not above them at all
I'm heading back to my bivouac
Returning tomorrow with more bombs from God

Bombs from God -- will create peace
Those lives sacrificed -- will be measured by God -- not me

Kent State Murder Day

```
A                                      C        G
```
Bombs from God cleanse the Earth -- of our enemies by birth
A Nazi, Communist -- or some kind of filth
Now to be silenced -- now to be stilled
Bombs from God bless their land
The future -- will be free for sure
Until some politician declares "War!"

Bombs from God are the answer -- to our fear
Bombs from God will be the -- voice they hear
Bombs from God will -- heal with pain
Bombs from God ARE JUSTICE! -- "LET IT RAIN!"
Bombs from God -- I'm just a button -- told what to do
Bombs from God -- Justice -- is our business
Bombs from God erase -- their evil empire
All who die will be purified -- by fire

Written 5-26-2014 by Coyote in his Toyota Tacoma covered wagon.

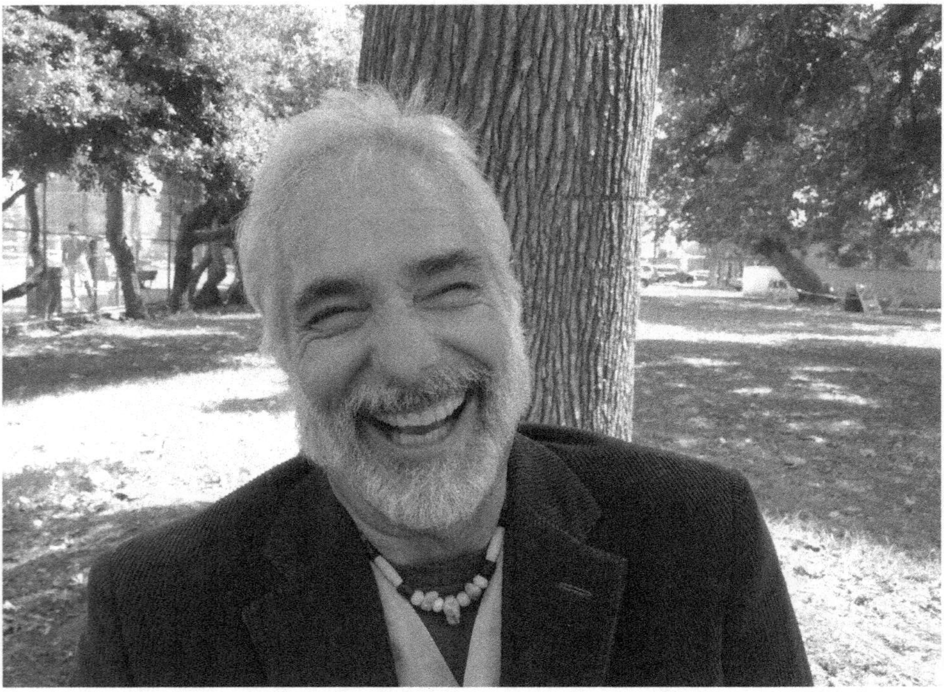

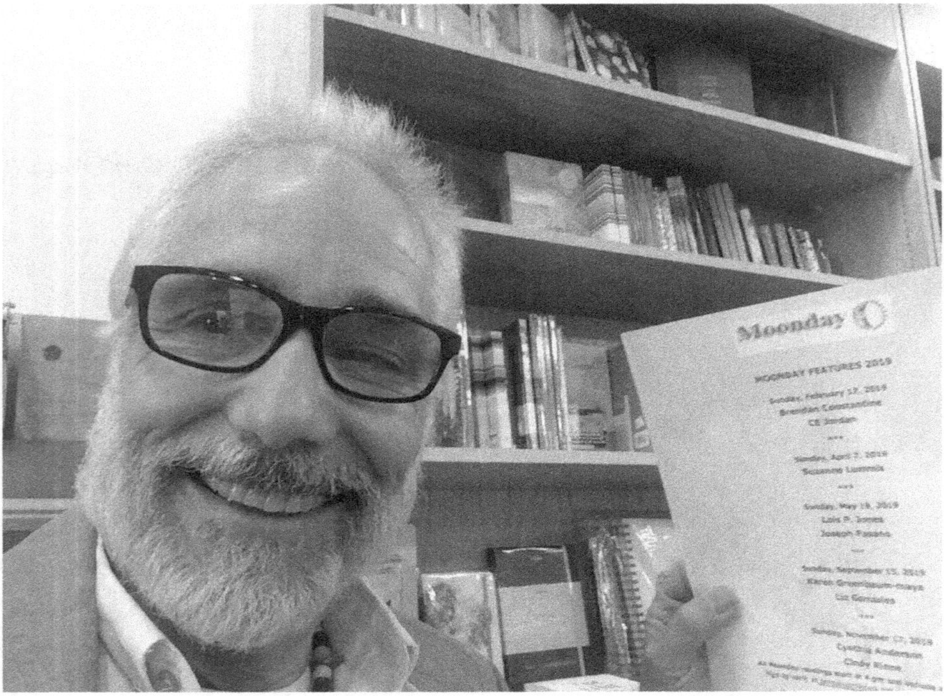
Moonday
MOONDAY FEATURES 2019
Sunday, February 17, 2019
Brendan Constantine
CE Jordan
Sunday, April 7, 2019
Suzanne Lummis
Sunday, May 19, 2019
Lois P. Jones
Joseph Fasano
Sunday, September 15, 2019
Karen Greenbaum-Maya
Liz Gonzales
Sunday, November 17, 2019
Cynthia Anderson
Cindy Rinne

5
BUDDHA Z BUDDHIST RAPPER

August 2019. I've been living in a homeless shelter for a year. Well, you are not allowed to say, "I live here." You are not allowed to call it a home. On a moments notice they can evict you. No recourse. No complaining.

There were four of us in that shelter room August 2018 when I moved there. Over the next few months all three of them were thrown out on the street to be homeless again. So I had the pleasure of rooming with more drug addicts than I'm willing to remember. There was a crybaby biker ...

During that year my stand up routine was evolving. I was the "Philosopher Poet." But I've always been a Buddhist. When I was at UCLA in 1985 or 1986 I discovered a book on Buddhism in the UCLA book store. I told everyone, "When I discovered what Buddhism was I discovered I was already a Buddhist."

Point is, during my years of poetry readings and wanting to make people laugh, I wanted to make people smarter. I wanted people to have better lives and become better people. That's why I'm famous as Shaolin Kung Fu master. Not because I've kicked asses or chopped off arms with my swords—because I make people happier. I make people healthier too. That's a big part of being happy. When you feel good, you're happy.

Back to that "point." My poetry started to become more Buddhist. Maybe it was always Buddhist, but after a few years I had A LOT of Buddhist poetry. I was becoming frustrated with not being able to be the Kung Fu Cowboy. I couldn't sell records. I couldn't form a rock band. I couldn't get on the radio.

So I stopped performing with my cowboy hat. I started performing in a suit with a vest and wearing Italian leather shoes. I was the "Poet: Sean Connery."

But I'm not sure Sean is a Buddhist.

I really want to build my online Shaolin Kung Fu school. I am Buddha Zhen. I want to have students. I want to make videos so I can improve people's lives when I'm dead. So promoting Buddha Z may be promoting Buddha Zhen. Who is Buddha Z?

Lots of things and worlds and people and realities came and went and were the places I was and people I knew. In the homeless world I was with convicts, drug addicts, prostitutes, junkies, thieves, stupid people, mean people, evil people, ignorant people, selfish people, manipulative people, lost people, artistic people, hard working people, government cheated people, generous people, and people who had made mistakes … like me.

I just wanted, want, work, and strive to be a better me. A more successful me. A dreamer whose dreams come true. A planner whose plans worked out. A strategist who is smarter than anyone I've ever known. I have faith in me. I believe in me. Despite where I am, I know I can be a billionaire. But like a successful farmer, I need a farm. Like successful record company I need employees. Like a successful movie producer I need to hire a few dozen people. As a homeless person—my dreams are just dreams. I need seeds for my farm. I need cows. I need land. I need a house.

So "Richard Del Connor Philosopher Poet" was a plan I could achieve. I achieved it. I made it to the top of the open-mic career. Now where?

Perhaps I could get noticed as a Buddhist Poet, playing Shaolin Flute. Philosopher? I am great. I am a wiseman. I am a philosopher. I am a poet. But who cares? Philosophy? I don't know anyone pursuing philosophy. No one. Not much of a market nowadays for wisdom. Millennials think they're smart because they have a smart phone. I remember one of them telling me, "My generation is smarter than your generation because I have every library in the world in my pocket."

Idiot. I had to walk a mile to the library when I was a kid. I had to use the **Dewey Decimal System** to find a book, and I learned more than these 'Brain in their Pockets Pokémon Pedestrians.'

Buddha Z? Well, like I said, over a few years of performing my poetry a lot of it was about Buddhism. A bunch of them were about the *"4 Noble Truths of Buddhism?"* So many of them, that I just published the first of 8 books teaching, explaining and illuminating the *"4 Noble Truths."* You can't be a Buddhist without learning the *"4 Noble Truths."* You can't achieve enlightenment without the *"4 Noble Truths."* The *"4 Noble Truths"* are the foundation of Buddhism. Every sentence of Buddhism was and is created to master and utilize the *"4 Noble Truths."* A noble purpose. Now I was doubly motivated.

I would be Buddha Z. I would share and enlighten people with my *"4 Noble Truths"* poetry.

I uploaded the book to Amazon. The **4 Noble Truths Explained — Book 1 of 8: Original Buddhism of India** is ready to be sold. Buddha's birthday is April 8. My plan is to start advertising the book on April 8, 2023.

I was excited to be Buddha Z. I was beginning my promo and marketing and planning to wear my blue Kung Fu uniform with white frog buttons …

Then the Covid-19 Pandemic stopped my performance career dead.

So I spent 2020 making Kung Fu videos, recording music, making podcasts …

Then I got cancer.

Check it out. Write me a good review.

Richard Del Connor

4 Noble Truths Explained by Buddha Z

From "Richard Del Connor the Philosopher Poet" he changes his poetry performances into "Buddha Z the Buddhist Rapper."

This poetry is a combination of those two poetry identities as this 8-book series began to enlighten audiences in Hollywood and NoHo. Want to be smarter? Want to be happier? Want to be enlightened? Dig in.

Book 1: Original Buddhism of India

Book 2: Noble Truth #1 - Life Includes Suffering

Book 3: Noble Truth #2 - The End of Suffering

Book 4: Noble Truth #3 - How to End Suffering

Book 5: Noble Truth #4 - How to Live Without Suffering

Book 6: Being a Bodhisattva - The Path to Nirvana

Book 7: Being a Buddha - The Path to Somewhere

Book 8: A Life of Meaning - The Path to Here

Book 1 of 8: Original Buddhism of India
from ShaolinCommunications.com

Shaolin Communications

As you can see, there are eight books in this series. It is my life goal to make sure that every American has an opportunity to understand what the **"4 Noble Truths"** are. Anyone who understands the **"4 Noble Truths"** can understand what Buddhism is.

I would like to guarantee that anyone who reads all 8 books will **"BE ENLIGHTENED."**

What is the translation of "Buddha?" Oh yeah, "Enlightened Person."

A world full of Buddhas. Heck. I may actually **"End All Wars™"**

www.BuddhaZ.com

"Shaolin Flute?"
Well it's not "Pussy Flute."
I used to challenge flute players to contests.
When I was homeless I'd play every day for years.
I was at my best.
I reached a peak.
I was in a movie.
But I didn't have an agent, a manager, a record company.
I wasn't on television. I wasn't ... well I was where I was.
Bummer.
Well, I enjoyed listening to my flute playing.
I'd play in parking lots and enjoy the echoes.

I played every time I read my poetry.
Some of the theaters sounded magnificent. A natural echo.
I got lots of claps. Lots of compliments.
I made some videos in my car and in the parking lots.
See if you can find them on YouTube.

"Great Salt Lake"
https://youtu.be/37inr2cLjfo

"Black Hills Ride"
https://youtu.be/3tRs0HLj_LI

Kung Fu Cowboy Channel
www.youtube.com/channel/UCHOBt22kW0K-79ePMxE9LMQ

Oh yeah. "Buddha Z — BUDDHIST RAPPER"

Well, as I started to say a couple pages ago, in 2012, 2013 and in 2014 there was a weird thing going on with black people. Somehow, they all believed they were rappers. It disappeared in 2015. But during those first years of my homelessness I would see two or three rappers a day walking down the street, rapping.

A convertible full of pretty black girls and a couple BMWs would park on the street. Someone would have a boom box with some beats on it, sometimes they were even recording it ... and someone would start rapping. His friends would be excited. People would be clapping. There were rap stars on every street in North Hollywood. It was like the 1960s when the guy at the park would Eric Clapton jamming with Stevie Winwood ... "Itchycoo Park" was a lifestyle back then.

I thought it was cool. I knew a dozen black guys who believed they were rap stars. I don't like rap music because I don't like the lyrics or the rappers. But I like a good beat and I like poetry.

So I wrote some poetry JUST FOR THE RAPPERS. But they didn't want to read any rap. They wanted to just jam it. They never wrote anything down. They would have a few main lines they'd remember and fill in the gaps. It did demonstrate that some of these black guys were clever and could've been poets—if they'd write it down.

I tried to write something the rappers would appreciate. Violence, drugs and pussy were the themes of all these wandering wonders. So I wrote the most cynical, resentful and angry poetry I could muster up. I wrote the lyrics up real neat and carried them around for a couple years trying to find a rapper to rap my rap lyrics. It never happened.

So in 2015 I gave up. I decided to record them myself.

These poems were too vulgar and resentful to be "Buddha Zhen" the Shaolin Kung Fu Zen Buddhist Master.

So I became Buddha Z. Sounded like a rap name.

I was actually afraid that Homeland Security would panic and arrest me.

But after carrying these poems/lyrics around for a couple years, I couldn't figure out what to do with them. They didn't really fit within any of my poetry books. They were too hostile.

So I recorded them with HEAVY METAL GUITARS. I was inventing the ZOMBIE THREE band and decided that would be the right sound for MY RAP MUSIC.

www.ZombieThree.com

I'm not sure what to do here, now, on this page.

I decided that my little half-hour poetry show may not be enough to be a "book." So I decided to add some more chapters to it. I wasn't planning on adding my Buddha Z Rap… but I was planning on sharing my "Buddha Z Shaolin Flute" identity that was aborted by the Covid-19 Pandemic Lockdown Shutdown.

So……… do I?

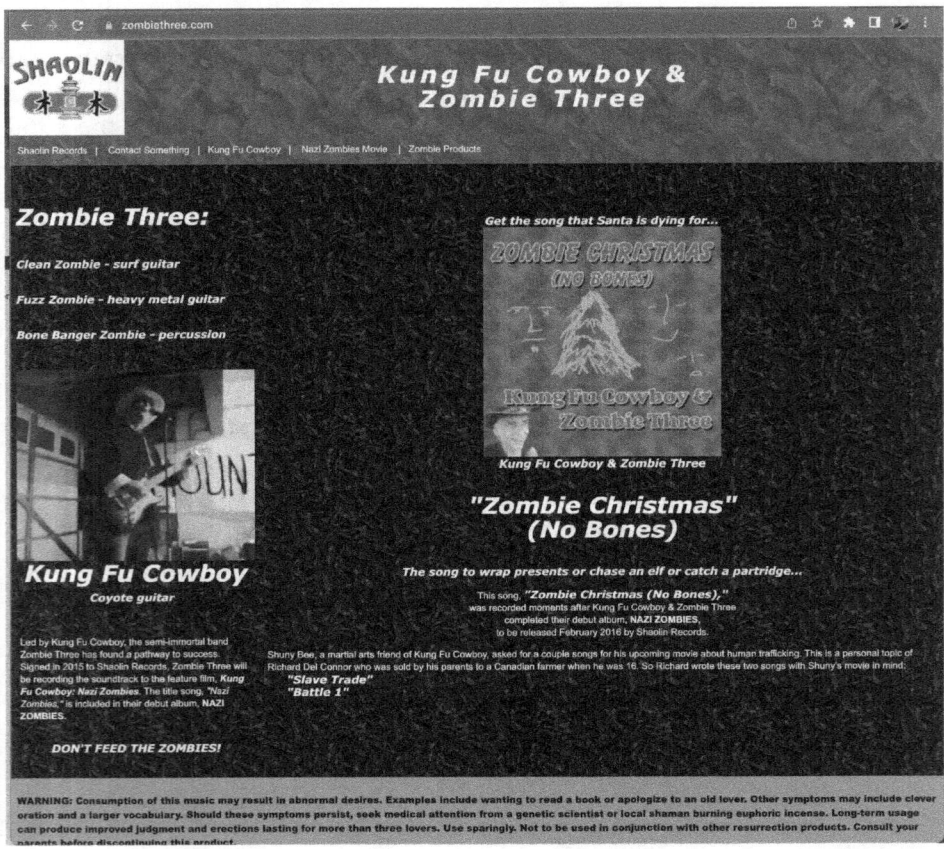

I just grabbed this screenshot of the Zombie Three website.

It's 2:30 am so I can't listen to music very loud. I plugged in my headphones and I'm listening to the *"Slave Trade"* song sample on this page.

I LOVE THIS SONG!!!!!!!!!!!!!!!!!!!!!!

I'm blasting it in my headphones.

DO IT.

I'm getting teary eyed. I WANT TO PLAY GUITAR.

I want to PLAY GUITAR LOUD.

I want to be on a stage with other musicians and my Marshall amp.
Why?
Why can't I perform?
I love to play music,
The tears are burning my eyes.
I want to play guitar. *$&^%^%$*@(@)$*$&%&Y%*@(!)_!_)

Now for the song, **"BATTLE 1."**
I hope I'm wrong. This may only be a partial song. I hope it's the whole song.

This Zombie Three band is my Buddha Z band.
I am the Kung Fu Cowboy on lead guitar.
FUZZ ZOMBIE is the obvious very distorted heavy metal guitar.
CLEAN ZOMBIE is a little bit cleaner on rhythm guitar.
BONE BANGER ZOMBIE plays BONES!
Yeah, he'll play drums too. But HE WILL PLAY BONES!

Bummer, this is the partial song. It just ended. I love this "Battle 1" song. I wrote FOUR ZOMBIE SCREENPLAYS and these songs have places in the screenplays. Sometimes when I hear these songs I SEE THE SCENES in the movies I wrote.

I wrote these Zombie Screenplays in 2015 when Zombies were IN FASHION. I could've rode that wave. I could've been opportunistic.
No money.
Homeless
No connections.
No band.
No agent.
No manager.
No record label.
No publicist.
No press.
No fan base.
No support.
No helpful friends.
No musician friends.

I live in a world of poverty. Not just money poverty—love poverty, friend poverty, support poverty, entertainment connection poverty, music business poverty, family poverty, and luck poverty.
HOW AM I SO HAPPY? How could I be so happy and have a smile

on my face with so much to complain or resent or miss or lack or need?

It sucks to be Zen. My first wife Raquel said, "You'll never be successful because you're too happy with what you have." I always hoped she wasn't right.

I'm a STOIC. Marcus Aurelius was the father I surpassed. I found the peace of mind and personal success he desired. Even the love of my family for a few years was better than anything he had or hoped for.

It really sucks to be a Buddha. Buddhists were supposed to be homeless and content without material possessions. The only material possessions I've desired were the items and technologies I needed to complete and create what I imagined and wrote and heard in my mind.

Oh yeah. Back to "Buddha Z Buddhist Rapper."

I probably haven't finished the webpage. Let's see. I'll go grab it.

Buddha Z — Buddhist Rapper

ShaolinRecords.com/RecordStore-R/BuddhaZ/buddhaZ-rap_artist.html

4 Noble Truths ALBUM by Buddha Z

ShaolinRecords.com/RecordStore-R/BuddhaZ/BZ-4NobleTruths.html

Do I? Well ...

The first album by Buddha Z is the ALBUM: **4 Noble Truths of Buddhism**.

I only have four songs written and performed I think. The songs need bass and drums to be completed.

One song has two rap versions back to back. I like that. You hear the same song twice, but a little different. I like both versions. I haven't listened to those songs in many years. But I think my plan was to release the album with that one song recorded twice. It's a long song I think.

Let's dig it up. (Appropriate expression for ZOMBIE SONGS.)
First step. COMPUTER FOLDER: ALBUMS of Shaolin Records
ALBUM FOLDER: BZ_1-4NobleTruths album
ALBUM ALBUM FOLDER: ALBUM-BZ1-4NobleTruths
PROJECT FOLDER: 1_Rough_Draft-BZ1
There they are. Each song has its own folder.
Top folder: 4 Noble Truths of Buddha

(Interesting. I thought it was supposed to be "4 Noble Truths of Buddhism")

It appears I've created an Adobe Audition project folder and imported all the guitar tracks and vocal tracks that I recorded in my car.

But I don't dare fire it up. Then I'll want to record the drums. Then I'll want to record the bass. Then I'll want to mix it. Then I'll want to master it. Then I'll want to go to the next song …

I made myself a kind of promise. I said, "I'm going to publish all my books before I go back to being a musician." It's not bad for me to bounce around between writing books and producing albums … but I'm at the end of my life it seems. I have to use my time wisely. I have to finish ALL MY PROJECTS.

I can write a book faster than I can edit, proofread it, edit it, create the graphics, create the formats, create the promo and ISBN registrations and copyright filings …

I've got to stay away from my music.

Well, it looks like this is more than an album. Here are the songs ready for completion:
"4 Noble Truths of Buddha"
"7-11"
"A Buddha Once Said"
"Assassination of a Tyrant"
"Bruce Lee in the Pokey"
"Buddha Z Anti-Rap Rap Song"
"Carol"
"Gotta Get Me a Dog"
"My Mistake"
"No Draft No Resister"
"Nuke DC"
"The Pound"

Yep. There's plenty for an album here. Perhaps a couple items that won't be on the album.

Here's the controversy. ***"Nuke DC"***

That song, "Nuke DC," was the main poem I wanted to find a rapper for. I didn't want my name associated with it. TOO CONTROVERSIAL. Very violent poem.

Hmmm. Eventually, I will deal with this album. It's ready to go. The tracks are here, ready to go …

After carrying my Buddha Z rap song, *"Nuke DC,"* in my pocket for a couple years in 2013 and 2014, I was liking the name, "Buddha Z."

So my 2013 memoir is titled, **Supersoul 13 — Discovering the Soul of God** by Buddha Z.

It tells the story of my almost making/producing/acting in my first movie: **Kung Fu Cowboy: Rock & Roll Movie 1**.

Check it out. I'm getting tired. It's 3:12 am now. Bed time.

I just noticed I'm still wearing my headphones.

I just found a rough mix of *"4 Noble Truths of Buddhism."*

It's a shame that I'm not sharing this with the world. Perhaps some people or teens would be enlightened with these three guitar tracks and a vocal. No bass. No drums. But it's cool.

Okay. I'm opening up the website, *www.CoyoteRadio.TV*

I'll upload to the song to the blog posts.

Hold on.

I just uploaded the song.

Now I have to create a blog post and link it ...

Hold on.

I did it. It's 3:33 am. So it took 21 minutes to post a song.

www.CoyoteRadio.TV/blog/

It's a new morning. Not necessarily sunny and romantic, yet free, independent, and self-determined.

This book, Kent State Murder Day, is to remind people each year on May 4, the anniversary of the Kent State College Shootings, that government should not be created or allowed to diminish free speech that aspires to change or improve that government. A parent will make rules preventing the children from stepping into the street. Eventually though, the children will be capable of crossing that street safely without parental supervision. So rules must evolve. Perspectives must be constantly reevaluated as new information is introduced. Decisions must be made that protect their children yet allow the children to possess their own decision making powers as they become capable.

As a parent I know what it is to make restrictive laws that as much as they protect my children also minimize my stress and concern. This must also be constantly reevaluated so that laws don't merely protect the status quo by shackling creative minds. Laws that one day protect a person can be stifling or unjust on a later day.

Part of the problem may be in dogma. I just looked up that word. Dogma is a, "Principal or set of principles laid down by an authority as incontrovertibly true."

Let's break that down. "A Principle." Principles are concepts that will defined, perceived, or lived by according to each person's perspective, environment of training. "A Principle" is a fundamental truth or proposition of truth that is the foundation of a belief. Wow.

That word can be a disaster. We all live by our principles, but in fact, we all live by only a few principles.

A single "principle" can enhance one's life or enslave it to ignorance. Yikes. My mind is spinning and churning through so many ideologies and religions and politics and slogans ... Wow.

Could this one word be as much a failure as a success of each person?

Let's look at some examples together and see where we end up.

My dictionary lists some examples.
- A peace plan that includes a ceasefire.
- Banks entitled to withdraw loans as necessary
- Refusing to pay a fine, on principle
- Foundation for a system of belief
  - Jesus = divine
  - Jesus = Son of God
  - Jesus = God
  - Jesus = born to erase sins of humans
  - Jesus = sacrificed (killed) for human benefit
  - Jesus = raised from the dead
  - Jesus = has supernatural powers
  - Jesus = walks on water
  - Jesus = makes more fish jump into fisherman nets
  - Jesus = creates zombies from dead people
  - Jesus = returning to kill all humans
  - Mohammed = divine
  - Mohammed = spirit who grants power to kill
  - Mohammed = someone to kill for
  - Mohammed = wants people to be killed who don't like him
  - Jews = chosen people of God
  - Jews = guaranteed by God a country to claim
  - Jews = allowed to exterminate people in their way
  - Jews = only a Jew if your mother was a Jew
  - Christians = believers in words of God
  - Christians = believe Holy Bible = words of God
  - Christians = killers of those who disagree with Holy Bible
  - Christians = killers of Muslims
  - Christians = killers of American Indians, "heathens"
  - Christians = decide rules of behavior for non-Christians
  - Christians = going to Heaven

- Christians = not going to Hell
- Christians = believers that non-Christians are going to Hell
- Communism = evil
- Communists = okay to kill
- Communists = people who disagree with Republicans
- Communism = destruction of USA
- Capitalism = anyone can be wealthy
- Capitalism = the rich people will provide for the poor people
- Capitalism = destruction of environment for financial profit
- Capitalism = enslaving people for corporate wealth
- Capitalism = freedom from Communism
- Capitalism = greed over generosity
- Capitalism = wealth controls the government
- Family = husband and wife creating children
- Family = male husband rules female wife
- Family = any group of people striving to help each other
- Family = only those of born lineage
- Family = only created by people of same race
- Family = only created by people of same religion

I'm getting tired. I could go on for hours. I look at the list in my mind and I cannot see the horizon, or rather, the list disappears as it exists beyond the horizon.

I need to think for a minute. "Principles."

Ouch. What about this principle, "I or We know what's best for You." Or, "You are not capable of making these decisions so We will make this decisions in your best interests."

That would be the government principle of keeping the discovery of aliens a secret from the world. A bunch of people in the government think they are fulfilling the duties of their job by keeping secrets from the people they work for.

Or what about the nuclear bomb principle of, "We need nuclear bombs to protect ourselves from other people using nuclear bombs to kill us." That principle has led to— hold on I'll Google that.

In 2022 there are 12,705 nuclear warheads in the world. Wow. One nuclear bomb can destroy a country. 90% of these atom bombs belong to the USA and Russia. So if the USA has 500 nuclear bombs ... why not stop when we had 10 bombs? Oh yeah, that "PRINCIPLE: atom bombs will protect us."

Why didn't the USA stop making nuclear bombs when we had 100 atomic bombs? Oh yeah, that principle, "Atom bombs will protect us."

Why didn't the USA stop when we had made 200 atomic bombs? You guessed it: "Atom bombs are created to protect us."

Why didn't the USA stop making atomic bombs when we had 300 bombs? Time for that "PRINCIPLE" again. PRINCIPLE: Atomic bombs keep us safe from people using atomic bombs against us.

According to Google, "A single nuclear bomb can destroy a city and kill most of its people. A nuclear war between USA and Russia would kill hundreds of millions of people."

So because we have "THE PRINCIPLE: Nuclear bombs protect us," we have created enough bombs to kill hundreds of millions of people. We have decided to kill every single person on this planet to protect ourselves. Is there any human reading this who does not see HOW RIDICULOUS THIS IS?

So our "PRINCIPLES" can lead us to "WORLD DESTRUCTION."

Wow. "Principles" are obviously the curse of this planet. "Principles" are the foundation of evil even when people think they are good people protecting good people with good intentions.

My mind is spinning again with "POLITICAL PRINCIPLES."

Wow again. Let's get back to the origins of this book, "**Kent State Murder Day**."

What was the "PRINCIPLE" for soldiers shooting protesters? They were protecting something or someone? They were not under attack. So the soldiers did not kill in self-defense. Killing someone to protect yourself is a basic human principle. Were the soldiers killing students to protect other people being threatened with death or harm by the students? No. From all reports, the students were non-violent. They weren't even threatening to harm anyone.

So what "PRINCIPLE" inspired or motivated the soldiers to shoot the young unarmed college student protesters? Well, the students were complaining about the government bombing Cambodia. This was an illegal act of war by the USA government. I'm not an expert on the Vietnam War, but my understanding was that the North Vietnamese or Chinese were trying to supply their North Vietnamese troops with food and weapons with a side route through Cambodia. I may be wrong, but let's use that theory to test our "principle."

Of course that principle of killing people trying to help our enemy is based on the principle that North Vietnam was an "enemy" of the USA. Ouch. That principle may be huge problem. How did we determine that North Vietnam was an "enemy of the USA" and that we could indiscriminately kill them accordingly?

I could Google again, but let's go with what the USA Government told me back in the 1960s when I was a teenager. By telling the United States newspapers and television news shows what the truth was, I was told this truth: "North Vietnam is a Communist country. And that North Vietnam wanted South Vietnam to be Communist country."

That's it. I heard that dozens of times from television news reporters and what little I read in the newspapers. I don't think they offered any other explanation. Well, actually they did: they said, "If South Vietnam became a Communist country that the United States of America would suffer or end."

Hmmm. These people in the USA government are the experts in world politics. They understand politics better than us common folk. They have the best advisors and smartest people in the country advising them. So, if we are killing people in Vietnam to protect the USA, it makes sense. Right? There is some kind of moral and legal right to kill people if your life is threatened. Right?

So the government said that Americans need go to Vietnam to protect us from death. It must be death. Communism means nothing to me. Meant nothing to me then. I couldn't explain its history or ambitions.

Oh yeah, the Government cured my ignorance. They explained that, "The goals of Communism are to kill Capitalism."

Okay. Self-defense of Capitalism makes murder justifiable and legal? Right?

Uh, what's Capitalism?

"Capitalism is freedom."

Well that's easy to understand. The government is protecting Capitalism to protect my freedom. Hooray for the USA military! They are killing people to protect me.

That's probably where most people stop asking questions. That answers all their questions and justifies all their murders.

So back to those soldiers on May 4, 1970 who are protecting the Kent State University from the students yelling and screaming about a war in Vietnam and Cambodia that is protecting America from Communism. I'm working real hard to understand the PRINCIPLES of people's minds in 1970. Don't forget, those soldiers are like policemen. They've been trained to obey orders, kill on command, and not question authority.

In the animal mind, a moment is reduced to me and you. Us versus Them. My job versus you getting in the way to do my job.

What did I believe in 1970? Well, I was completely indoctrinated by the news and newspapers and my parents. So if they believed the war in Vietnam was a good idea, then I should respect the opinions, understandings, knowledge, wisdom and PRINCIPLES of my parents. Right?

Wrong. Somehow, I knew this war was wrong. None of this information about Communism and Democracy and Government and Vietcong and Evil China impressed me as true. Maybe 10% true. But there

Kent State Murder Day

was no doubt in my mind that none of those arguments above were substantial. I was unconvinced. I was incapable of standing on a podium and changing other people's minds, but my mind sensed that all this huffing and puffing and political fear mongering was somehow corrupt or dishonest. I was ignorant, but perceptive. When I was exiled to Newfoundland in 1970 I got an ulcer. That's a wild story about how I got that ulcer. But I had an X-Ray in 1971 that showed the scar tissue of my Duodenal Ulcer. I had the Newfoundland doctor give me a copy of that black and white film image and his doctoral report of how it could easily recur and my being more susceptible to future ulcers than a "normal" person. I treasured that manilla folder as my last chance effort to avoid any military service so that I could avoid being drafted into the Vietnam war. I knew many Conscientious Objectors and Military Deserters in Canada who preferred their being fugitives in Canada than soldiers in Vietnam. They didn't influence my decision, but they strengthened my resolve.

All right. It's about time for me to make dinner so let's wrap up this huge exploration into the world of "PRINCIPLES" with a final perspective.

It's 2022. We did not conquer North Vietnam. We did not prevent North Vietnam from infiltrating South Vietnam. South Vietnam became a Communist country. Okay. All our USA fears were realized. Everything we fought for failed. The United States is doomed. They've assured us of that. Hundreds of our USA Senators and Representatives and Military Officers have assured us that under these circumstances America will suffer. We sacrificed thousands of lives and billions of dollars to prevent this. America is doomed. South Vietnam has become a Communist Country.

I've lived in America since 1974. I've witnessed the fall of Capitalism. I've experienced the suffering of the USA from South Vietnam becoming a Communist country. I should be weeping and sad that we did not prevent this. Right?

Wrong. I can't think of one single day since 1974 when I thought or said, "I wish we would have won the Vietnam War." NEVER. I've never thought that. I've never said that.

Hold it. That means that our USA Presidents were wrong to support that war. That means our entire government was wrong to support that war. That means that all the military advisors were wrong to support that war. That means that millions of Americans were wrong to support that war. That means we wasted millions or billions of dollars on an unnecessary war. That means that a million people died unnecessarily because of an unnecessary war. That means that a million people suffered from wounds and trauma and destruction of their property and businesses and homes because of an unnecessary war.

My mind is sad. I don't want to continue this enlightenment. How can I summarize this huge mistake that caused death, loss, injury, destruction, famine and evil?

Sorry. I don't want to cry. I'm going to make my dinner.

This chapter was supposed to be about my evolution from "Richard Del Connor Philosopher Poet" to "Buddha Z Buddhist Rapper" in 2019 when I performed my poetry show as "FEATURED POET" in a North Hollywood theater on May 4.

In my mind, the transformation was midway. My poems were becoming completely Buddhist in subject matter. But I was still wearing suits with vests and maintaining my "Philosopher Poet" image until my last performances in October 2019 when I obtained an apartment using **"Section 8"** and ended my homeless life.

I haven't performed onstage since then. 2020 began the Covid-19 Lockdown. Today, November 17, 2023, as I write this page, I've lost my desire to be in public places. I order my groceries online and go to a designated area of the Walmart parking lot to have them pushed out to my car and loaded up outdoors.

Each month I visit an Albertson's Customer Service to obtain my monthly rent money orders. But I always wear a mask.

If I performed onstage, I could not wear a mask. If I performed in a library or theater, I would probably be breathing the exhales of my audience. If one single person in the audience has Covid-19, there is a high probability that I will contract the disease. I have evidence of this from friends and relatives attending a restaurant dinner and everyone contracting the disease from one person who knowingly showed up with the Covid-19 virus.

At first I believed I am capable of surviving and developing an immunity. But this self-confidence has been diminished. Worst yet, my relatives have complained of several months of lethargy and limited mental capacity after becoming healthy.

The thought of me operating at a reduced intelligence is especially frightening to me as I publish my books right now. I wish I was smarter. I definitely don't want to be dumber.

So podcasts and videos are the way for me now. Same with Kung Fu classes.

Kent State Murder Day

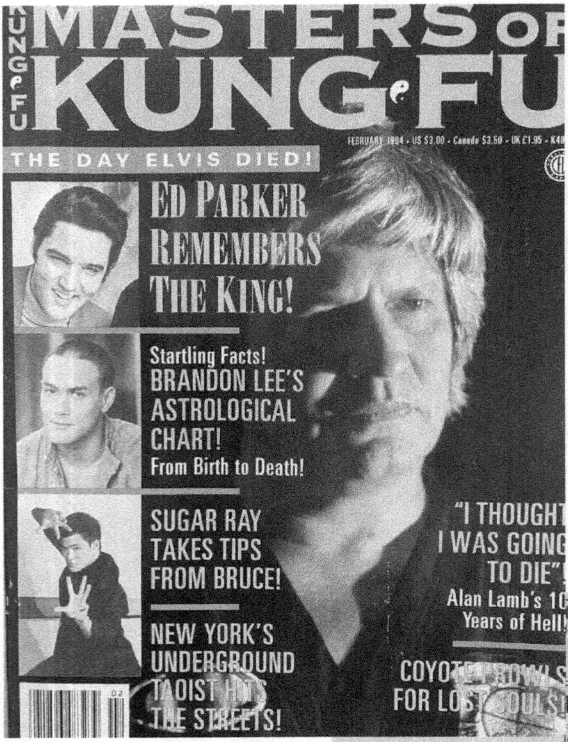

COVER STORY

Ed Parker Remembers the King

Friend, bodyguard, teacher, confidante. Ed Parker was all those things and more to The King. Right up until the day Elvis died. *By Ed Parker*

14

FEATURES

6 A Black Belt's Leap of Faith
Andre Alex Lima had always been curious about the inner strength ... provided. He decided to put it to the test by jumping from the third floor of a ... *By John Corcoran*

14 Coyote on the Loose
Richard O'Connor, nicknamed "The Coyote", has found a home for his myriad talents in the wide-open spaces of Utah. *By Michelle McCarty*

20 Sounds from the Underground
Frank Allen, New York's resident underground martial artist, is taking his message to the street. *By Clarence Lu*

26 Inside the Life of Brandon Lee
According to one astrologer, even if there had not been an accident on a movie set, Brandon Lee's fate was sealed from birth. *By Patricia Noxera, with David L. Wilson*

KUNG-FU MASTERS (ISSN 1060-7645) Editorial offices: 4201 Vanowen Place, Burbank, CA 91505, (818) 845-2656. Return postage must accompany all manuscripts, drawings and photographs submitted if they are to be returned, and no responsibility can be assumed for unsolicited materials. All rights in letters sent to ***Kung-Fu Masters*** will be treated as unconditionally assigned for publication and copyright purposes and as subject to ***Kung-Fu Masters'*** right to edit and comment editorially. Contents copyright © 1994 by CFW Enterprises, Inc. Nothing may be reprinted in whole or in part without written permission from the publisher.
Kung-Fu Masters is published monthly by CFW Enterprises, Inc., 4201 Vanowen Place, Burbank, CA 91505. Printed in U.S.A.

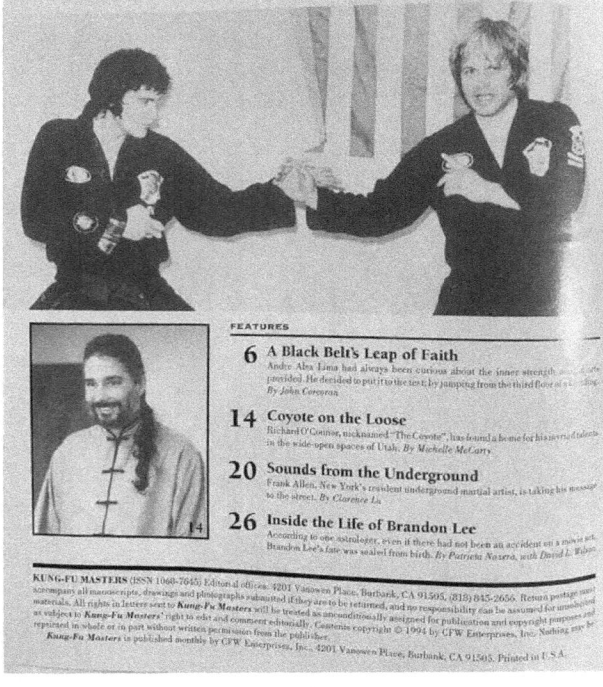

Kent State Murder Day

Buddha Z poetry performances?
Buddha Z rapping?

www.BuddhaZ.com

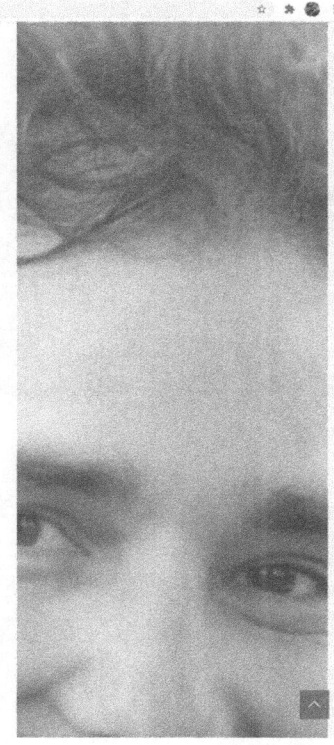

"It wasn't until a bassist friend of mine asked me to help him kick his drug habit that I realized the potential of tai chi chuan."

3 Wisdoms of China

All three are philosophies WITHOUT gods.

Kent State Murder Day

Online Tai Chi Youth CLASSES

Buddha Z is completing the **Shaolin Chi Mantis Beginner Program** video classes. There are 350 videos for 350 classes and about 90 videos to go.

When the **SCM Beginner Program** is completed at www.ShaolinInteractive.com we will seek funding and begin the 600 videos for the **Tai Chi Youth PROGRAMS**.

However, Buddha Z wants to start the Tai Chi Youth classes or at least some sort of **Tai Chi Youth Program** RIGHT NOW, March 2021, even while making the SCM class videos. Today's youth have less opportunities for sports and exercise than any other time in the last 50 years. We have perhaps THE BEST possible exercise program to offer youth and young adults WITHOUT ANY SPARRING and no broken bones since 1984 when Buddha Zhen began teaching Shaolin Kung Fu and Yang Tai Chi Chuan.

So we will offer LIVE TCY Online Classes by ZOOM. Buddha Zhen has taught 8 of these LIVE Zoom classes so far, and kind of has a handle on the Zoom class concept. We've figured out in the last week how to record the classes on a computer while teaching the classes using his iPhone 11 phone/camera to teach the Zoom lessons.

So far this has been challenging and disappointing with adults complaining "This is more exercise than any other Tai Chi class..." Most people in America have NO IDEA what real Tai Chi Chuan is. The Yoga teachers and Karate instructors have put "Tai Chi" on their store windows to capture the ignorant Americans who think that Tai Chi Chuan is an "easy, relaxed, slow moving exercise for old people in a park or YMCA."

They are wrong! **Tai Chi Chuan translates as "Supreme Ultimate Boxing Style."** If you cannot beat up anyone and everyone with your Tai Chi you've been scammed and cheated by someone who didn't have any business teaching whatever it is they claim to know. Tai Chi Chuan is a fantastic self-defense IF YOU ARE TAUGHT TO DO IT FAST.

Buddha Zhen raised his kids with Tai Chi Youth classes.

Plus, your instructor has to know HOW to use the Tai Chi moves for self-defense. Since 1992 our students have visited other Tai Chi schools and reported back to us their disappointments.

Shaolin Chi Mantis Traditional Buddhist Kung Fu and Taoist Tai Chi Chuan is the parent school of Tai Chi Youth nonprofit education organization. If your instructor is not teaching you Taoism they are a fake, a fraud and are cheating you out of your time and money.

So, we've decided to leave all the Tai Chi scammers alone, and stop arguing with the American Tai Chi students who don't believe in doing kicking exercises and pushups... to ONLY teach YOUTH classes to persons 13 to 20 who have not been poisoned with "Yoga Tai Chi." Young adults from 20 to 29 will be allowed in our online classes if they are WILLING to learn REAL TAI CHI and Shaolin Kung Fu. The combination of Shaolin Kung Fu and Yang Tai Chi Chuan have been proven by Buddha Zhen in prisons, rehabs, public schools, YMCAs, YWCA, church programs and public parks to improve the health, well-being and self-awareness of hundreds of young students. Most students will even see their public school grades rise dramatically while students of our Tai Chi Youth programs. Unfortunately, we've also seen the grades decline after they quit our Tai Chi Youth programs. So stick with it. After the first semester you will have a complete understanding of what Tai Chi Youth and Shaolin Chi Mantis have to offer you and what is expected of you to succeed in our programs.

6
TEENAGE HIPPY - VIETNAM WAR

Kent State Massacre
Kent State Shootings…

4 killed

9 wounded

Soldiers aimed their guns at students.

Students unarmed.

Soldiers fired rifles and pistols at USA students.

Soldiers tear gassed students.

Older Generation condoned attack.

Younger Generation protested attack.

Older Generation of WWII support war.

Younger Generation denounce war.

Us versus Them.

Us = counterculture.

President Nixon says he's not listening to protestors. Dick says he's listening to the "Silent Majority."

I was living in St. John's, Newfoundland from May 1970 to June 1972.

Canadians despised President Nixon. They wore T-Shirts with a drawing of Richard Nixon and a huge SCREW in his chest.

People disliked me for being an American until they'd find out I was from California. Then they figured I must be cool.

In 1972 I turned 18 in February and the FBI started looking for me as a "Draft Dodger."

I was living on a boat. I was homeless.

I decided to hitchhike back to San Diego, California.

In 2015 I launched a fundraiser online.

I wanted to capitalize on my exile to Newfoundland story.

I attended seminars, watched videos and talked to all my friends. I was still pursuing financing for my movie, Kung Fu Cowboy: Rock & Roll Move 1, so I had accumulated movie business contacts over the past few years. I consulted them and they gave me good advice.

I warmed up as many people as possible. I create release forms so that I could interview people and include them in this documentary and memoir.

I promoted the fundraiser asking for at least $3,000 to cover plane fair a month's lodging in Newfoundland to do some research and revitalize my memory with the sights and smells of St. John's, Newfoundland, where I lived from 1970 to 1972.

No one had a story to tell like this. How many people do you know were exiled from the United States?

How many people do you know who lived on a 60-acre game reserve and had to feed 600 wild ducks and geese gathered from around the world?

How many people do you know who had 7 snowy owls in their basement and an osprey?

How many people do you know who lived in a 4-bedroom farmhouse with their Biologist Professor Uncle in one room, six ravens in the next room, then their own room, and one more room as an office?

How many people do you know who had to fight off a pedophile uncle he was busted by local DDT investors who sought to destroy the game reserve because he worked for the WHO World Health Organization and had succeeded in banning DDT use in Newfoundland. Some people lost a lot of money on that DDT company investment. They retaliated and destroyed the game reserve after sending the RCMP Royal Canadian Mounted Police to execute all 600 of the wild fowl.

In the United States they were executing college students. In Canada they were eliminating environmentalist college professors. I became homeless, as an American exile in Newfoundland, Canada, in 1971. I was exiled to Newfoundland, Canada, in May of 1970.

This is the farmhouse I lived in on the 60-acre Oxen Pond Game Reserve founded by my uncle, Dr. Richard E. Warner.

The left side stairs led up to that porch. When I lived there the porch just had a railing without windows or screens. I would sit on that porch and play my uncle's classical guitar and sing along to songs I knew and songs I started writing. This was the beginning of my songwriting career.

Another professor at MUN Memorial University of Newfoundland, had a reel-to-real Teac tape recorder. I began recording my original songs and jamming to my blues compositions. I still have those tapes. I need a 1/4" tape recorder for those recordings. I need a few other tape machines for my 4-track, 8-track, 16-track, and 24-track recordings from the 1970s and 1980s.

Hundreds of geese would gather at sunset everyday and completely fill this backyard. They would listen quietly as I played and sang. As soon as I would stop they would raise their heads, point their beaks to sky and honk, cackle, and voice their applause. It was amazing. These ducks and geese were my first audience as a rock 'n' roll blues composer performing artist.

Kent State Murder Day

On May 4, 1970 the Ohio National Guard fired bullets into college students in a non-violent demonstration at Kent State University. They were protesting the Vietnam War and Cambodia Campaign of illegal bombing by the United States Government and Military Industrial Complex. We were bombing huge areas of another country because they wanted a different type of government than the USA had.

3.1 million Americans were shipped to Vietnam to kill people of all ages.

BAD GUYS:
130,000 North Vietnamese CIVILIANS killed
849,018 North Vietnamese MILITARY killed
250,000 North Vietnamese MISSING IN ACTION
600,000 North Vietnamese MILITARY WOUNDED
1,000   Chinese KILLED
4,200   Chinese WOUNDED

TOTALS of "Bad Guys":   NORTH VIETNAMESE:
1,100,000   KILLED / MISSING.
  604,000   WOUNDED

GOOD GUYS:
   300,000   South Vietnamese CIVILIANS killed
   300,000   South Vietnamese MILITARY killed
 1,170,000   South Vietnamese MILITARY wounded
    58,000   United States MILITARY killed
   303,000   United States MILITARY wounded
    15,000   Laos MILITARY killed
     5,000   South Korea KILLED
    10,000   South Korea WOUNDED
       521   Australia KILLED
     3,100   Australia WOUNDED
       351   Thailand KILLED
        37   New Zealand KILLED

TOTALS "Good Guys":   USA and ALLIES:
  300,000   KILLED.
1,300,000   WOUNDED
1,000,000   CAPTURED

TOTAL HUMANS KILLED for USA Government goals:
1,300,000

The farther boat in this photo was a 35-foot "trap skiff" when I moved to Newfoundland. An empty canoe fishing boat. My uncle hired a local Newfie shipbuilder to build this cabin on it. This was my first carpentry job. Besides building this boat five days a week, I had to feed the ducks and geese twice a day.

We finished the boat before they destroyed the game reserve. My uncle hired me at $25 a day to work on the boat as an assistant biologist studying tide flows, and pollution from a lumber yard.

During the winter I would have to stand on the bow of this frozen slippery deck and push icebergs out of the way with a gaff pole. If I fell in the water my uncle said I would have 30-seconds before the icy water sucked my heat and energy and stopped my breathing. We had to navigate snowstorms with a compass … I don't want to live on a boat ever again.

Kent State Murder Day

What were the GOALS of our USA Government from 1964 to 1974?
How did the USA Government benefit from these GOALS?
How did the USA country and society benefit from 1,300,000 being KILLED in Vietnam?

What did we learn from killing one million people in Vietnam?
Under what circumstances should we kill another million people?
If the USA Government kills another million people, should our USA National Guard shoot them for protesting?

P.S. In 2001 and 2002 I was insulted by friends and family whenever I suggested USA NOT GO TO WAR or ship soldiers to the Middle East. It appears that the television, media, and YouTube videos determine whether Americans want to kill people in other countries.

On May 4, 2018, I was the "Featured Poet" of the North Hollywood monthly poetry performances at a small theater. As I prepared for my 25-minute show I realized this was the anniversary of the "Kent State Massacre" of college students protesting the Vietnam War. I was 16 years old on May 4, 1970, and had participated in antiwar marches and as a young hippie was part of the flower power counterculture.

So I decided to dedicate my "Featured Poet Show" of "Richard Del Connor Philosopher Poet" as "Kent State Murder Day." I organized my existing poetry that I'd written in the last couple years criticizing the Military Industrial Complex, USA Politics, and printed my handwritten lyrics and poetry into a libretto that I printed up for my performance audience. This book contains these poems and copies of the original handwritten libretto. I was homeless at that time and performing more than once per week in various open-mics, poetry readings and book fairs as, "Richard Del Connor Philosopher Poet."

I would like to keep this "Kent State Massacre" alive as a reminder to future generations as part of my own antiwar activities. I hope you find this inspiring.

In 2021 I spent the year in cancer surgery, chemotherapy, and cobalt radiation treatment. I wasn't sure how long I would live and created the AMERICAN ZEN PEACE FOUNDATION to continue my antiwar writings, websites, and my music albums and books.
www.AmericanZenPeaceFoundation.org *"End All Wars™"*

Richard Del Connor

Here's another photo of the boat I built. I have many memories of living on this boat. Many of them were horrific, frightening ... and it never held still. I lived on it for days at a time.

I was willing to revitalize my memories for my book, Boy She Kept. But I couldn't raise enough money to pursue this book while I was homeless in 2015. It seemed that no one wanted to hear my amazing stories, or know what it was like to be in a world of pedophiles, television producers, college professors and wealthy car distributors.

Because it involved international human trafficking, the Homeland Security, and several USA Government Agencies and their attorneys persuaded me to abandon this project since in also involved the Canadian Government.

War can only be stopped by the common people, convicts, and vengeful killers. The Government makes money off every war everywhere. I believe that ALL WARS are bad and created by bad politicians. It's up to you. I'm doing more than anyone I know.

I spent most of my time building my first DAO for Tai Chi Youth.
<u>https://app.SuperDAO.co/tai_chi_youth</u>

The SuperDAO company is in Russia. They helped me set up my DAO for free in 2021.

This was before the Ukraine War. I was assured that because my Tai Chi Youth DAO web3 website is on the "blockchain" that it can't be taken down during the Russian War with Ukraine.

I hope they're right.

The war started as I was just finishing launching the NFT fundraiser and establishing the DAO Treasury and Membership …

You need METAMASK in a Chrome Browser to login to this website.

Join the Tai Chi Youth DAO and support my nonprofit online school.

These THREE NFTs are to run the online school of Tai Chi Youth.

This Kung Fu School TEACHES NONVIOLENCE. It works!

That first summer I lived on this 60-acre game reserve I would go down to this private lake of ours called, "Oxen Pond," and go swimming all by myself. The bottom of the lake was a thick mush. At worst I thought it was duck and geese poo-poo. That winter I was informed that all of the homes around the game reserve ran their sewage lines into this pond.

Even my best memories are soured.

I would take the German Shepherd named, Moose, on walks around the game reserve through the forest. It was cool, spooky, very dark with clouds blocking the moon. A flash light made it worse. My son commented to me once, "You're never afraid dad." Perhaps I'm more fearless than I realize.

There are packs of wild feral dogs in these woods and no Dog Catchers out here. These dogs would attack cars on the dirt and gravel roads every day. They were a nuisance. Sometimes they would travel in the forest about 20-yards away from us. Without that huge, and very violent German Shepherd those packs of dogs would've attacked me. Moose killed one of them and almost killed a neighbor's dog. He bit me when I pulled him off that dog and I had to beat him up. We were best friends after that.

Kent State Murder Day

Buy an NFT for you and someone else too. Please.
These painting NFTs by Richard Del Connor are for fundraising and donations. We need to hire video editors and web designers to build the online school. I am about to start the 900 videos for a 5-year program of NINE SEMESTERS and a 2-Year instructor training program.

I can CURE NONVIOLENCE. I've taught in prisons. I have proof.

https://app.SuperDAO.co/tai_chi_youth

This is a self-portrait from when I lived with Sally Kuehn and her two kids. I wish my hair grew this fast now. It grew about 12" in one year.

I was hired as the bassist of a band, Lukey's Boat, in St. John's, Newfoundland. I was thinking about that band the other day. I was meek, humble and didn't complain. I didn't have a musical ego yet. I was a session man, or session boy at age 16 and 17. They were a "Classical Rock" band with very classical, Beethoven style rock songs. I wasn't happy. Too bad I didn't push my music on that band. Maybe we could've accomplished something since all the other musicians were ten years older than me.

So I formed my own blues rock band with Wayne "Ab" Stockwood called, DOGMEAT. We were both Frank Zappa lovers and had that anarchistic rebellious attitude. He was my best friend in Newfoundland. I tell the story in one of my books I published this year about a riot we caused at a high school dance we performed at.

Kent State Murder Day

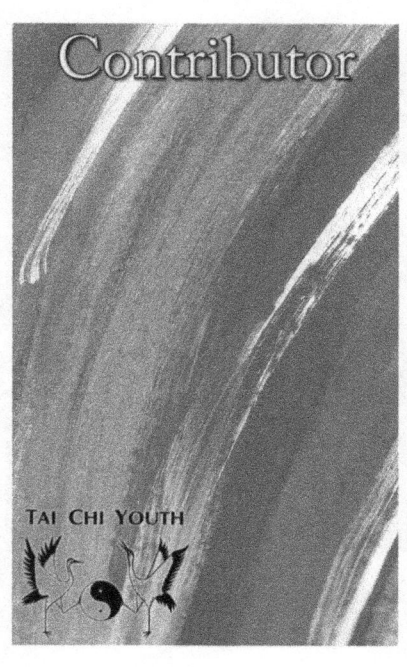

I wish I'd learned this Tai Chi Youth program when I was a teenager.

Semesters 1 to 3 = White Sash
BEGINNER LEVEL.

Semesters 4 to 6 = Yellow Sash
INTERMEDIATE LEVEL.

Semesters 6 to 9 = Orange Sash
ADVANCED LEVEL.

Semesters 10 to 13 = Red Sash
INSTRUCTOR LEVEL.

Students learn the Yang Tai Chi Chuan short form of Shaolin Chi Mantis which has improved and saved many lives since I began teaching it in 1984.

I am right now setting my up living room Kwoon to film these 900 videos. I've been purchasing hard drives, lights and editing software.

I've started building an online school for my Shaolin Chi Mantis traditional Shaolin Kung Fu Buddhist online school. I've shot 200 of the 320 videos before I got cancer. Rather than finish this program I'm going to film the Tai Chi Youth videos first.

www.ShaolinInteractive.com/courses

50 weeks x 4 classes = 200 classes = one year.
1 semester = 16 weeks.
9 semesters = 144 weeks
9 semesters x 16 weeks x 4 days per week = 576 classes/videos

So 576 classes = entire Tai Chi Youth program = Tai Chi Masters.
I have to video/edit/upload/and create a webpage for 576 classes.
I have been fundraising to hire help: video editors, webmasters to help me build the online school with the 576 classes …
Please help me if you can.

www.TaiChiYouth.org/donate

www.AmericanZenPeaceFoundation.org

I have started building a DAO for the American Zen Peace Foundation.

As I mentioned earlier, **SuperDAO.co** is a Russian organization. I was told that there were not concerns about being locked out or losing my DAO …

https://app.SuperDAO.co/american_zen_peace_foundation

If you can help finish making this DAO,

or want to help me END ALL WARS™

Join my DAO.

7
AMERICAN ZEN PEACE FOUNDATION

American Zen was and is. In 1992 when I realized that Utah was not what I hoped for— When I realized that my photography careers was destroyed, left behind in Hollywood, California; I sought to create a rock band in Utah. I couldn't. My backup career and financial backup/bail out had been Union Carpentry since 1972. This was gone in Utah. My movie career, making commercials, music videos and working for Hollywood Special EFX companies was no longer possible. I could not create a rock band in Utah, the Mormons would not allow it and there were only three clubs in Salt Lake City to perform in.

I was given a 4-track tape recorded by one of my students. She also bought me a drum machine. So I created the American Zen band and pretended to be all four band members. I am:
- The Hippy Coyote — vocals, acoustic guitar, flute
- Rory G — electric guitar, slide guitar
- Tom Calder — Rickenbacker bass, Vox organ
- Steve Hixon — drums

Richard Del Connor is the RECORD PRODUCER of all American Zen albums and I'm also the recording engineer.

The first two American Zen albums were recorded and released in the mid 1990s. I sold them to friends and students. I manufactured them one at a time by creating a CASSETTE MASTER and duplicating it. I hand labeled the cassettes and autographed them.

Then I recorded the first album by BUDDHA ZHEN. I had been performing Chinese New Years events and festivals on flute and Chinese pipa (a 4-string lute). So I recorded an entire album of my original Chinese folk songs used for our Shaolin Chi Mantis Demo Team. Some songs are appropriate for meditation. The album was released in 1996 on cassettes, recorded on my 4-track recorder.

This first Buddha Zhen is titled, *Tai Chi Magic 1*.

In 2001 I got ProTools after moving back to California. I converted the

4-tracks of the **Tai Chi Magic 1** album into ProTools and added some more tracks of music to some of the songs. I released the **Tai Chi Magic 1** CD in 2009. I handmade all the CDs one by one and sold them to friends, students and some Yoga teachers at the YMCA where I taught Tai Chi Chuan classes.

As a Kung Fu and Tai Chi master I am Buddha Zhen.

As a heavy metal Buddhist Rapper, Buddha Z is a sassier version of me.

American Zen is neither of these dudes. When I'm in American Zen I'm THE HIPPY COYOTE. I can smoke pot and talk about my LSD hippie adventures. My other identities are a little more respectable.

To complicate things a little more, I decided that The Hippy Coyote could retire in 2014 when I completed the last American Zen album, **LEVEL 8 = End of the Line.** Since The Hippy Coyote always had long dark brown hair, it also made sense to let my new silver hair identity be The Kung Fu Cowboy.

www.KungFuCowboy.com

So yeah, I still believe in ending all wars. Not just the standard beauty pageant slogan. I really believe that. Why do I believe I can end all wars?

First of all, it would be nice to get people, any people, any person, any adult to believe that a world without war is even possible.

Well, I'll have to bypass that obstacle. People are stupid. People like watching war movies. People like watching television shows about war. Kids play with toy soldiers. Scientists are paid good money to invent new bombs, new planes, new jets, new drones, new tanks, new rockets, new cannons, new rifles, new pistols, new bullets …

There are thousands of people making soldier uniforms and rations and backpacks. They don't want to lose their jobs.

There are lots of people making those planes, tanks, jeeps and supplying gas and tires …

So despite all the simple minded common folk who actually get excited about other people suffering—that doesn't leave many humans on this planet to inspire my belief about a world without any wars at all.

So rather than fight that uphill battle of persuading people to even consider a world without wars—my plan is to make people less violent. Change people's ways of thinking.

I discovered when I was teaching in prisons and drug rehabs that if I can make people feel good they are happy.

When I make people happy they are more friendly.

When I make people more friendly they are more sociable.

When I make people more sociable they are more compassionate.

When I make people more compassionate they are more generous.

When I make people more generous they are less violent.

When I make people less violent they are less inclined to promote war.

If I can make many people less inclined to promote war—I think they will inspire other people to not believe in war.

That's what I can do.

Help me make the Tai Chi Youth online school. The future has a chance.

Oh yeah. I figured out a way to improve politics. The truth is, all those Military corporations bribe all the congressmen to create more wars—as many wars as possible. The Senators and Representatives are all bribed with millions of dollars to promote and create more wars.

So I figured out a way to minimize our government supporting the Military Industrial Complex. Create a new government. The American Government is a swamp of liars, cheaters, crooks and war mongers.

I created a BRAND NEW GOVERNMENT to **END ALL WARS**™.

This **"USA 3 Party System"** will focus on the future of our planet a lot more than any government on this right now.

USA 3 Party System

Republican, Democrat, Libertarian… all = discontinued.
No memberships transfer to any new party.

SKY PARTY   Space, Infinity, Spirituality
EARTH PARTY   Land resources, Animals, Humanity
WATER PARTY   Oceans, fresh water, Ecology

All parties headquartered in Washington, DC
Senators = 5-Year Term. No re-election in all Executive Government.

People's Referendum:
    If political process = gridlock (Congress Houses)
        1. Public Debate = One Month = Month #4
            a. Political figures (Week #1)
            b. Public figures (Week #2)
            c. General public of each party (Week #3)
            d. Senators Revote (Week #4)
        2. If political gridlock still exists: (Month #5)
            a. Political figures debate
            b. Public figures debate
            c. General public each Party debate
            d. Senators Revote
        3. If political gridlock still exists   (Month #6)
            a. Political figures debate
            b. Public figures debate
            c. General public each Party debate
            d. PUBLIC VOTES

USA 3 Party System

I published a couple books in 2012 under the pseudonym, Rachel Connor.

My friends told me that proposing this "USA 3 Party System" would be more than controversial. I have a bunch of other government ideas that would improve the world and probably get me assassinated.

So I decided to publish my government improvements under a pseudonym, Rachel Connor.

I even had feminist ideas and published a book titled, **Putting Men in Their Proper Place**. No one has given me a review of that book, but I think it will piss off everyone. Yeah, probably everyone. I published it as Ebook with an ugly cover. I'll get to republishing and updating it.

In 2012 I had death threats and I was stranded in Las Vegas. It was even worse than I thought. I was beginning my homeless life that would last until 2019. I didn't get killed but I lost more than I would have dreamed of. I'd like to think—well, let's just hope there are a few people I never ever see again.

That Las Vegas fear was useful I writing the four Zombie-Vampire screenplays that take place in Las Vegas. It's really a shame I'm so poor and have no connections in the music or movie business. I could make a lot of people a lot of money if they would give me the opportunity to make what I can make.

Oh yeah, I can END ALL WARS™ too.

Richard Del Connor

Music NFTs of
American Zen LEVEL 1

American Zen ALBUM: LEVEL 1 = Peace Of Mind
https://OpenSea.io/collection/american-zen-level-1

Shaolin Records OpenSea Account
https://OpenSea.io/ShaolinRecords

American Zen

What is American Zen?

I thought I answered that question earlier. Hold on. Hmmm. I just scanned backwards and saw some information about the LEVEL 8 = Memorial Day album.

Perhaps I'm remembering the last book I published. Hold on again.

The last book I published was Sid's Place, by Richard Del Connor.

Page xix begins a breakdown of my albums and books created. That's a good start.

Page 309 starts my "Discography." Some more good information.

But now, let's see if I can explain it even better.

I committed myself to travel an 8-LEVEL spiritual journey. I could only guess what that spiritual journey was. I made a basic outline.

LEVEL 1 = family success. Reproduce and be happy.
LEVEL 2 = add religion to family and business life.
LEVEL 3 = accept all religions and befriend all races = compassion.
LEVEL 4 = help other people be healthy and happy.
LEVEL 5 = help your community or city.
LEVEL 6 = help the world and have a spiritual path.
LEVEL 7 = graduate the material world and know where Heaven is.
LEVEL 8 = bridge / access / connect to the spiritual world without dying.

That was my plan outline. Be a successful animal in LEVEL 1 and be a successful soul in LEVEL 8.

I started in 1991 and graduated my spiritual journey in 2014. If I hadn't been so poor, homeless, isolated and lacking friends, family and creative fulfillment—I could've graduated or reached LEVEL 8 sooner. Poverty slowed me down.

For each of these 8 LEVELS of spiritual growth and development I created an album and at least one book.

That's a brief summary. How I accomplished these 8 LEVELS of spirituality was unique to my life and my ambitions. Someone else would accomplish these 8 LEVELS in their own unique way. So my goal isn't to lay a specific path as much as I should be INSPIRING YOU TO PURSUE AND ACHIEVE YOUR spiritual growth in your own way.

Each of these 8 LEVELS is awesome and of course unique. So everyone should appreciate my Shaolin Zen Buddhist spiritual journey as something worth investigating BECAUSE YOU CAN'T DO what I've done.

I have webpages, albums, books and NOW I have NFTs that I will create sell for each LEVEL. These NFTs are valuable because of the stories, links and information I supply in the "Description" of each NFT. Plus, you should want to collect them because I am one of the most talented, interesting, and inspiring person in the world. Did I say that? Well, I can't dispute it. Can you?

Music NFTs of
American Zen LEVEL 2

American Zen ALBUM: LEVEL 2 = Christ Killer
https://OpenSea.io/collection/christ-killer

Shaolin Records OpenSea Account
https://OpenSea.io/ShaolinRecords

What is a Christ Killer?

There are several answers to that question. MY first answer would be: people who stifle their creativity or compassion. That unique talent that's inside you should be nourished not leashed/squished/and restricted. A Christian might say we all have a little Christ in us. After all, how else can you walk in Christ's footsteps and live by his peace and love ideals?

My second answer would be people who regularly celebrate the murder of Christ. Anyone who is happy about Christ's murder is a Christ Killer. If Christ came back you'd celebrate whipping, stabbing and starving him to death again. Yuck. Christ Killers. It's hard to believe that people could be so stupid to support killing a human because they think they'll get a better place in Heaven or have their sins erased.

When people stop thinking that killing ANY human is a good idea—we will be a big step closer to not killing people in other countries because we don't like what they are thinking in their mind.

Do you know how many Christians have been killed by Christians because they didn't agree with what the priests were preaching? One flavor of Christianity believed that God and Christ wanted them to kill other Christians. And that another flavor of Christianity believes that God wants them to kill people who are not Christians. Is that really what Christ would want if he was alive today?

My third answer about Christ Killers are the people who make rules that limit the lives and happiness of other people because they believe that's what Christ wants them to do. They believe that killing or making rules or punishing other people because then those limited rule obeying people will live a better life even if they disagree with you.

So I think there are many types of Christ Killers.

This **Christ Killer** album by me was inspired first by an incident in musical instrument repair shop. I was getting my flute repadded. I teenager came in with a clarinet. I think he was getting it serviced, but after what the repairman told me, it may have been to sell it. The repairman told me, "It's such a shame. That boy is a gifted musician." Obviously I needed more information so he explained what I was still learning about as a new member of Utah Mormon civilization. "That boy is going on his Mormon Pilgrimage." (Sheesh. I forgot what they call it.) "When they go on this Missionary Missions they are not allowed to play any musical instruments for two years until they return home."

I learned that Mormons have to sacrifice their teenage sons and daughters to become "Missionary Elders" for two years. They knock on doors and cannot live with their parents. They have to live in special homes owned or rented by the Mormon church for two years selling Jesus door to door, full time, without any other education, or entertainment, music study. I thought of that as a "CHRIST KILLING" practice.

Wanna save the world?

We need to END ALL WARS™ first.
Contact me.

www.americanzenpeacefoundation.org/contact/

Contact Me

Be healthy and happy.
   www.ShaolinInteractive.com/courses

Help me create my online school for the Tai Chi Youth nonprofit.
   www.TaiChiYouth.org

Help me create, run and manage my Tai Chi Youth DAO.
   https://app.SuperDAO.co/tai_chi_youth

Help me create and run my American Zen Peace Foundation.
Do you really want to miss the opportunity to END ALL WARS™ ???
   www.AmericanZenPeaceFoundation.org

Help me build and run the American Zen Peace Foundation DAO
   https://app.SuperDAO.co/american_zen_peace_foundation

Help me run my independent record company.
   www.ShaolinRecords.com

Help me run my music publishing company.
   www.ShaolinMusic.com

Help me run my book publishing company.
   www.ShaolinCOM.com

Help me make my Kung Fu Cowboy ZOMBIE MOVIES
   www.KungFuCowboy.com

Help me make movies and music videos.
   www.ShaolinPictures.com

Buy some songs from me.
   www.CoyoteRadio.TV

Richard Del Connor

We = Me (right now)

I'm an old hippie now. I resent using that word, "old," because I think I'm more youthful and energetic than most millennials.

How can I inspire younger generations to SEEK PEACE?

I'm hoping my AMERICAN ZEN folk rock band will be a way to connect to them. Using that connection I'm presuming they will befriend me, in an internet kind of way, and be influenced or enlightened by my hippie ideals.

To make American Zen even more influential I have built a business plan for the American Zen Peace Foundation to create a NEW AMERICAN ZEN BAND every 10 to 20 years of young musicians in their early 20s. Utilizing my Shaolin Records independent record company to record them and produce concerts, they will be able to mature through the 8-LEVELS of the American Zen journey as the record the songs I've written and travel similar paths through Buddhism, Taoism, Lakota Sioux Shamanism, Confucianism and Philosophy to inspire THEIR GENERATIONS to pursue and achieve enlightenment and Nirvana.

That sounds so cool. Help this to happen by American Zen Peace Foundation.

What Can You Do?

JOIN TAI CHI YOUTH. No one has ever complained and said they regretted attending these classes.

EVERY PERSON who has attended these classes has enjoyed them.

If you are reading this in the years 2023 to 2025, you may be able to still help me build this online school. Help! Right now, as I'm writing this in November of 2022, I am a one-man operation.

Join the Tai Chi Youth BOARD OF TRUSTEES. Right now I have a co-screenwriter and ex-wife helping me. That's it. I need webmasters, video editors, membership directors, promotion people, social media marketing… and I'm working for free after being homeless for six years. I need help.

But I'm moving forward.

Yesterday I was discussing the new Tai Chi Youth Online School CURRICULUM with my ex-wife Michelle. She has seen how our daughter benefitted immensely from the program during her childhood. So she is

supportive and a firm believer in what this program can achieve.

Please help me. I'll do it all by myself if I have to. But it will turn out better and the online school will be built faster if I can get some help.

Otherwise, just attend the classes. Purchase the semester memberships and IMPROVE YOUR LIFE. This is a MIND + BODY + SPIRIT program. If you can improve yourself, the future of humanity is improved. Be part of peace, happiness, well-being and better health on this planet. BE THE FUTURE.

Join the Tai Chi Youth WHITE SASH first semester.
www.ShaolinInteractive.com/courses

ABOUT THE AUTHOR

Richard Del Connor 1970

I was 12 years old in 1966 when I started 7th grade at Harvey J. Lewis Jr. High School. I gave up piano at age 10 for the trombone because my Uncle Richard had played trombone and he was my biologist and father role model. But in 1966, trombone wasn't cool anymore. I told my parents to take my trombone back to Ozzie's Music Store and get me an electric guitar. They traded in my trombone, but said, "We are not going to buy you an electric guitar." So I got a paper route until I could buy myself a red Fender Mustang electric guitar before I turned 13.

I also traded in my innocence for kissing girls in the bushes, smoking pot and dropping acid. As a performing rocker and blues guitarist, I had access to lots of drugs and hung out with musicians older than myself. I was a hippie. I was counterculture. I was flower power. I was peace, love and antiwar. After many episodes and altercations from the police for my LSD and pot usage, they finally caught me with a kilo while pointing a nervously shaking pistol gun barrel in my face and exiled me to Newfoundland in May 1970. That same month the National Guard aimed their rifles and pistols at college antiwar protesters in Kent State and pulled the trigger. I am an exiled hippie who publishes songs and poetry with the pseudonym, The Hippy Coyote. In 2014 I grew up a little when I realized my hair was silver and became the Kung Fu Cowboy of Shaolin Records. I'm also a Shaolin Zen master, Tai Chi master, flutist, bassist, record producer, recording engineer, journeyman carpenter, architect, novelist, and retired Mr. Mom.

Now I want to share what I know, illuminate what I've learned, and improve the future with my nonprofit, Tai Chi Youth, that has proven that teaching Shaolin Kung Fu and Yang Tai Chi Chuan with daily discussions of Zen Buddhism, Taoism, and Confucianism can make people smarter and reduce their violent tendencies. I've rehabilitated drug addicts, murderers, convicts, and improved the lives of seniors and kids. Watch me.

Kent State Murder Day
A One-Man Show May 4, 2019

I would like to make this an annual event. May 4, 2020, was Covid 19 Lockdown. Perhaps LIVE ZOOM, Facebook LIVE, or some other internet LIVE event would be fun. Help me. Plan this. I'll be there.

I am publishing this book May 4, 2023.

I need a car. I need a home. I need book sales. I published 22 books in 2022 at Amazon. I released them in KINDLE, PAPERBACK, and HARDCOVER. They are on the shelves. Now I need to figure out Amazon marketing and advertising. Again, I could use some help. I've watched some videos…

I will publish all my books in 2023 at Draft2Digital who will distribute them to Barnes & Noble and Apple Books.

I will then make audiobooks of my 30 books published. Then I plan to do more advertising…. Help!!!

I was hoping to be a musician this year in 2023, but I've got ten more books to publish and I've got several novels I keep chipping away at. I don't want to write any more books right now, but I wake up with these story ideas and have to write them down… I'm trying not to write a new book.

Although I've decided to hold off on being a musician another years, I keep waking up with songs in my head between 2AM and 4AM at least one night per week. I get out of bed and write out the lyrics. I get a red pen and figure out the chords and write them above the lyrics. Then I record it on my phone and go back to bed.

If I write the song earlier in the evening when I can sing louder, I will plug my guitar into my Marshall amp and make a video. I've posted a dozen of these on my TIKTOK account:

https://TikTok.com/@kungfucowboyclassicrock

It's impossible to be me. I can only be part of me each day. I WANT to be a musician. Today I bought some backgrounds and I plan to shoot some music videos this year.

I tell you all of this so you'll understand how difficult it is for me to pull off these annual **KENT STATE MURDER DAY** events.

Oh, another distraction. (Probably a CIA plan.). Every May 4 is NOW *"Star Wars Day."* What an ironic distraction or diversion. Isn't the *"Kent State Murder Day"* just a *"Star Wars Day"* in a future universe?

Perhaps the *"Star Wars Day"* events planners could invite me, rather me trying to compete with them. I represent the common man standing up the MILITARY INDUSTRIAL COMPLEX. Isn't that what Luke Skywalker did?

I'm going to finish editing this book today and publish it.

If you can support me, an artist, an antiwar activist, poor person… I'd appreciate it. I'm on **Section 8** getting a housing subsidy. I could lose it on a moment's notice and I'll be homeless again. Worse off than ever. My car ignition is busted. I had to get towed from Walmart a week ago, unable to start my car.

Help.

Better yet, just buy some of my albums:

https://www.ShaolinRecords.com

Buy some of my books: Amazon, Audible, or my website:

https://www.ShaolinCOM.com/booklist-S.html

I've got a few new websites I'm building for fun:

https://ScorpionResurrection.com

https://PsychedelicRockOpera.com

https://CoyoteRadio.TV

https://CoyoteRadioTujunga.com

https://BuddhaZ.com

Thanks for any purchases! That's my favorite way of being supported.

And don't forget I've got a nonprofit ONLINE school I'm building. Sign up and see if you can learn Tai Chi. You'll be glad you did.

https://shaolininteractive.com/course/tai-chi-youth-white-sash-class/

Tai Chi Youth WHITE SASH semester one teaches the first half of the Yang Tai Chi Chuan form of Shaolin Chi Mantis plus Kung Fu basics.

Can I play my cancer card for a little empathy? I spent 2021 in surgery, radiation treatment and chemotherapy. I'm trying to start my life over, while realizing my time is more limited than I ever considered. I'm 69 years old now. I've got to make 800 videos just for the 4-year Tai Chi Youth program. Help me out. Sign up. Join the school. Become a Tai Chi Youth instructor. I have enjoyed 40 years of being paid for making people healthier and smarter. I always do the workouts, so I'm smarter and healthier… Join TCY!!! I've lived a great life. You can too.

Call me, if I'm still alive. I love to share what I know: 818-723-2769

https://www.ShaolinCommunications.com

Bringing Light Online Since 1999™

www.ingramcontent.com/pod-product-compliance
Lightning Source LLC
LaVergne TN
LVHW041618070426
835507LV00008B/325